The
Uncomfortable
Truth
About
Racism

Also by John Barnes

John Barnes: The Autobiography

JOHN BARNES

The

Uncomfortable

Truth

About

Racism

HEADLINE

First published in 2021 by
HEADLINE PUBLISHING GROUP

1

Cataloguing in Publication Data is available from the British Library

Hardback ISBN: 978 1 4722 9038 0
Trade paperback ISBN: 978 1 4722 9039 7

Designed and typeset by EM&EN
Printed and bound in Great Britain by Clays Ltd, Elcograf S.p.A.

MIX
Paper from
responsible sources
FSC® C104740

Headline's policy is to use papers that are natural, renewable and recyclable
products and made from wood grown in well-managed forests and other
controlled sources. The logging and manufacturing processes are expected
to conform to the environmental regulations of the country of origin.

HEADLINE PUBLISHING GROUP
An Hachette UK Company
Carmelite House
50 Victoria Embankment
London EC4Y 0DZ

www.headline.co.uk
www.hachette.co.uk

To the greatest man who ever lived,

Colonel Roderick Kenrick Benedict Brindsley Barnes;

my father, a man of integrity, morality and honour,

who made me the person I am on and off

the football field.

Acknowledgements

I have so many people to acknowledge and thank, people who have helped me to finally get this book finished.

I write like I speak, fast and unstructured, so while all the words here are my own, I needed help with the structure, punctuation and format of the book, and so engaged with the people who understand me most.

First, my two sisters, Gillian and Tracy, who both live in America. Growing up, they were my vocal intellectual sparing partners from when we were aged eight, nine and ten, me being the youngest. I spent hours emailing them chapter after chapter so they could help with checks on spelling, grammar and punctuation, and provide advice for the first half of the book.

I think they got fed up with me constantly emailing and changing parts of the book regularly, so I passed their duties onto my first-born daughter Dr Jemma Barnes, who took it upon herself to go over every chapter by herself for the last two years, all the while working in her day job as a doctor, to make sure everything was right. Many times I would email her a piece of text to edit, and I would get a reply along the lines of 'Sorry, I'm in theatre doing an operation, but will do it as soon as I get out'. That shows her dedication to my book. This is a real family affair.

My loving wife Andrea was also an inspiration to me, as well as a wonderful sounding board. She was a calming influence throughout many of my rants about life, especially the all-too-frequent instances of discrimination and the establishment's insufficient solutions.

I have spent many hours in discussion with all of my grown-up children, the others being Dr Jamie Barnes, Jasmin Barnes and Jordan Barnes, talking about every one of the incidents and discussion points in the book, and their insights have been invaluable. We have watched and marvelled at how their little sisters and brother, Isabella, Tia and Alexander, have mirrored them in character and humility, and in understanding the good fortune of their environment whilst also having empathy for people less fortunate than themselves.

So my entire family have helped me over the last three or four years: watching them grow and become the people they are has fully convinced me that circumstance can determine outcomes if a stable, loving and encouraging environment can be provided.

I won't pretend that all of the thoughts in this book are original: the many authors of the countless books I have read on the subjects discussed have had a profound effect on me and guided my perception. Having said that, I have interpreted their books in my own way so the authors' intent may be misrepresented by me.

Finally, while my book is dedicated to the greatest man that ever lived, my father, they say behind every great man is a greater woman, and that greater woman is my mother, Frances Jeanne Barnes. She would regularly wake me up at six every morning from the age of twelve (which I hated!) to meditate and place subliminal positive messages in my mind about life. These messages sunk in, without me even knowing it at the time, to help me move my life forward. After her loving husband grew ill, she decided in her mid-sixties to become a barrister and is still practising in court in Kingston, Jamaica at the age of eighty-five. She is an example to us all of the resilience, love and fortitude necessary to live a complete life, and like my father she guided me every step of the way on my journey to where I am today.

CONTENTS

CONTENTS

Author's Note

Before you start reading, I want to make it clear that everything in this book is a representation of my thoughts and perspectives on all of the discussed topics. It is a completely personal view.

INTRODUCTION

At the start of my writing journey for this book many years ago, I was hopeful, excited, empowered, and had a real belief in the human spirit of right-mindedness, not only in the average person but in our leaders who wanted a better, more equal life for us all. Historically, Britain has always been influenced by the concept of social class: even its own parliament was structured on a class system, with the House of Lords representing the privileged upper class and the House of Commons representing the rest. I understood this class structure, which prevented real equality, and decided to focus on racial inequalities while also considering gender, sexuality and other issues, as they are all intertwined with each other due to our unconscious conditioning, a concept which I shall explain in more detail throughout the book.

There were highs and lows along that journey, with equal measure I'd say, but as time went on, I realised that for every step forward there were two steps back. This made me think about how people over the last few hundred years must have felt when little steps were taken in their situations, and whether they also thought things would get better in their lifetime. But those were the olden days and we are morally and intellectually superior to those people today, surely? I became increasingly aware that, arrogantly, we don't take into account that people in the past may have thought exactly the same thing about themselves.

I continued to prepare the book to its conclusion, which I hoped would herald a time for all of equality of opportunity (not necessarily 'equality of outcomes' as that's more nuanced due to class and other dynamics), with the future looking brighter for the next group of young dynamic activists helping to shape the debate. I'll let you, the reader, decide on whether we have come anywhere near that watershed moment.

•

All this seemed the furthest thing from my mind when I first set foot in this country. When my parents told me that we were coming to England, I was so excited – I was going to the home of football! I was two months past my twelfth birthday, and I remember landing at Heathrow in late January 1976 on a Sunday morning. On the drive into central London, I saw lots of organised Sunday youth team games with referees and linesmen and fully kitted out boys of my age. It was one of the coldest winters in recent times and while I had never experienced snow or cold like that, it didn't matter at all when there was football.

We moved temporarily into an apartment off Baker Street where we lived for a few months before we found a house in Golders Green, a very affluent, predominantly Jewish area in north London. The schools nearest to Baker Street were St Marylebone Grammar School for Boys for me, and for my sisters Gillian and Tracey, Sarah Siddons Girls School. St Marylebone was one of the few traditional grammar schools remaining in central London and had high academic standards. On the other hand, Sarah Siddons was horrendous, a comprehensive in Paddington, with girls from one of the roughest parts of London with a high incidence of undisciplined, disruptive behaviour, smoking and a poor academic level.. So, once we moved to Golders Green my sisters were taken out of that school and were sent to a well-regarded girls grammar school in Hampstead Garden Suburb called Henrietta Barnet School. Despite the move, I remained at St Marylebone and my parents drove me to school each day on the way to their respective jobs in central London.

Let me say that my parents were by no means snobs. Their upbringing in the '40s and '50s in Jamaica (for my mother) and Trinidad (for my father) was not one of luxury and privilege, but was a relatively middle-class experience by the standards of those times. The one thing they insisted on though, in the age after independence, was a good education. That being paramount in their thoughts, Sarah Siddons school wouldn't do for my sisters, but St Marylebone was fine for me. The one problem with St Marylebone was they didn't play football, only rugby.

It was a great school though, a 200-year-old grammar school with a difference. Its catchment area meant that it had a lot of boys from the inner city in attendance, and while it was probably rougher than your typical grammar school, the level of education and aspirations among most of its pupils was very high. Although football was not part of the school curriculum, that was all that was played in the playground. I remember clearly my first day at school, this Jamaican boy with a 'funny' accent, in a brown duffel coat, standing in the playground at first break, waiting to be picked by the boys who already knew each other. The hierarchy had already been established, as the other boys had started senior school the previous September while I arrived in February of the following year, five months later. I was last pick after a nerdy boy with glasses and a club foot (only joking, but not far off), but after fifteen minutes of play I was completely and wholeheartedly accepted in the cool gang from that moment on.

Our gang growing up in London was a mixture of Black and white kids. At school it was cool to be Black, or to hang around with Black kids, and we fully identified with each other. With my football coming on leaps and bounds, we obviously had to find a local club for me, and that came about through one of the members at my sisters' swimming club near Baker Street, who was related to a man who coached at a boys' club in nearby Paddington, Stowe Boys Club.

When I joined the club, it reminded me of my days in Jamaica playing in the rough inner-city areas of Kingston. My teammates were boys from the 'hood', and while at first they teased the grammar school boy, thanks to my ability, I was soon fully accepted at their club. Whereas most of the Black boys in my school were from working-class families who lived on council estates, the boys at Stowe were different. They may have also grown up on council estates, but the Stowe boys went to schools like Rutherford Comprehensive and Paddington Comprehensive, which were rough schools around the corner from St Marylebone. In years gone by they would have probably come to bully the 'posh' grammar school boys. But that didn't happen in my generation. I remember times when they used to come near our school and we would square off in our respective groups but nothing would come of it, the difference being that this 'posh' grammar school now had big, rough, Black kids representing it. So, instead of ongoing fights, a new level of respect was forged and friendships were made. The group identity among my friends from school and friends from Stowe was very strong, and race played very little part in our lives. Although, I was aware of the issues my Stowe friends had with police stopping them regularly in the areas where they lived.

Around the age of fifteen, I started to go clubbing and saw more of life outside of home and school. My school friends and I went to mainly mixed clubs (Black and white) where we listened to soul, R&B and rap music, while most of my Stowe friends went to reggae clubs which were strictly Black, smoky (not from cigarettes) and slightly scary to a middle-class boy from Jamaica. If you could play football though, you were fine.

Going out in London and mixing with different people from different parts of the city was fun, but there always was this perception of people from south London, east London, west London, etc. being 'different' from each other. Nonetheless, my school friends and I never felt intimidated or uncomfortable anywhere. As I said, the majority of the time we would go to our usual 'mixed' clubs. Every now and then we would go to 'white' clubs, but very rarely as a group would we go to 'Black' clubs. Sometimes, when the group was exclusively Black, we would go to Black clubs.

This is where it became very interesting. If, as a group, we went to a white club which was unfamiliar to us, my Black friends and I wouldn't feel uncomfortable in the slightest (unless there were skinheads or men with white hoods on), and my white friends wouldn't feel uncomfortable for us or feel that we felt uncomfortable. But if we as a group went to a Black club, I would automatically feel uncomfortable for my white friends because I knew they would feel uncomfortable, and I would feel the need to say to them 'you're alright in here'. Why was that? Why would my white friends who were just like me in terms of our 'identity' (not racial identity but we liked the same music, sport, television shows, etc. and dressed and spoke the same) not feel the need to reassure me that the white club we were in was okay, but I felt the need to reassure them that the Black club was okay?

While I didn't rationalise it back then, I've since realised that there had always been an unconscious perception among us all: that white culture and the white environment was non-threatening, moral, orderly and safe, and the opposite was true of the Black environment. So, although I knew that the Black club was fine, I subconsciously knew that some of my white friends, who despite hanging around with Black people all the time, nevertheless felt intimidated. They felt that way because THEY DIDN'T KNOW 'THOSE' BLACK PEOPLE!

How often have Black people with white friends heard them negatively speak about 'Black people generally', but finish off by saying to them 'not *you* though, you're okay'? I didn't know 'those' white people in the club either, but I felt fine, and my white friends also expected me to feel fine, because what was there to worry about? 'White people are fine', even if you don't know them.

•

Living in London, as I got older I was becoming increasingly aware of racial bias in the world due to experiences that young Black adults faced (as opposed to thirteen-year-old cool Black kids whose white counterparts hung around with them for street cred). Of all those kids from the '70s and '80s – Black and white – who hung out together and 'identified' with each other, socially, musically, the way they spoke, dressed, I wonder how many of them are still in contact or still identify with each other? If they don't identify with each other anymore, then whose identity has changed? I can tell you whose identity has changed: a lot of the white kids I hung out with, because of the young urban dynamic of that time, were perceived to be 'acting Black'. When you leave school and become an adult, where is that persona going to get you in a racialised world which has a misconception of Blackness? So, for the white intelligent kids who I grew up with, they could revert or 'become white'. But for a lot of the Black, equally intelligent kids I grew up with of the same identity as their white counterparts when they were young, they couldn't NOT be Black anymore.

So, if you look at the proportion of the white friends who I grew up with compared to the Black friends I grew up with, who were/are of equal intelligence, drive and aspiration, I don't need to tell you which group has been far more successful in life. And while my white friends, along with most people of unconscious and subtle privilege, will tell you that the main factor that contributed to their achievements is their 'ability' and no other circumstance; it's really not that simple.

I am categorically not saying that my white friends who have been more successful than my Black friends haven't absolutely deserved their success due to their abilities; but it hasn't been a level playing field for everyone. And I'm just lucky that I could play football, as I'm sure my acceptance and opportunities granted to me by society probably would have been very different if I didn't have this talent. For me, football was the gateway to what lay ahead.

PART ONE

'Man becomes great exactly in
the degree in which he works for
the welfare of his fellow-men.'
Mahatma Gandhi

1

LIFE AS A YOUNG, BLACK PROFESSIONAL FOOTBALLER

I signed for Watford at seventeen years old and my family had already gone back to Jamaica before I even had my first pre-season training session with the club. Although I had only been in the country for five years, thanks to my experiences in what some consider to be the most formative years (ages thirteen to eighteen), I suppose I felt English. So, going into what could be considered a harsh environment (an English football club in the early '80s) as a young, Black footballer, it could have been quite daunting.

I had witnessed 'racism' while growing up in London so was not naïve to its existence. But when I started playing professional football, it took on a whole new dynamic on a personal

3

level. I was shocked at first to hear and see my white team-mates 'abuse' their Black peers in training, only to then see that they were doing it in a jovial, tongue in cheek, almost friendly way. Then seeing my older Black teammates laugh it off and respond in an equally trivial way, remarking about their lack of dick size or the rhythm or coolness that 'we' had. This was commonly known as 'taking the piss'. The way that the Black and white players would trash talk each other reminded me of the old Black American 'your momma' jokes ('Your momma so fat she . . .', 'Your momma so ugly she . . .', etc.). No matter who was winning or who was funnier with their insults (and I'm not trying to get my former teammates into trouble or say I was in anyway upset by it, for it absolutely did make me laugh), everything ended, and the banter battle was always won when someone coolly and calmly stated: 'AT LEAST I'M NOT BLACK.'

Now, these were players who would 100 per cent have my back against white players of the other team when we went out on the pitch. In every meaningful way, they were/are my closest friends and in no way did they feel they were in any sense seri-ous about their comments, but they said these things because of what the world had shown them: that they had every right to feel superior and that any argument could be won with that type of banter. While I also felt/feel as equal and worthy as any of them (superior in some cases) I also unconsciously knew that they won the argument with that winning statement because of the world's perception, not of me personally, but of Black people generally (of which I was one). This wasn't a case of individual me versus individual you, it was MY PEOPLE versus YOUR PEOPLE.

Why should I be upset with a teammate when he is absolutely right in terms of what the world and society has untruthfully told him and continues to untruthfully tell him about his race in relation to mine? Instead, let's be angry and do something about the society that made him, and still makes people feel that way, unconsciously or not. What struck me as strange, was that some Black players accepted this argument-ending comment easier than others, and the ones who didn't were considered to have a chip on their shoulders. You have to remember, this was in the early '80s before political correctness, when racial abuse with no recrimination or consequences was an accepted part of society.

It was worse in the '70s when there were very few Black players, and those young Black players of the '70s who survived then became the mature Black players of the mid-'80s who were battle-hardened to the scourge of racism, because they had to be in order to survive. There was the odd Black player or two who wouldn't take any crap, and the white players were wary about such banter around them.

I was a young, Black professional footballer relatively recently arrived in England from Jamaica, witnessing and being subjected to overt 'racism' for the first time. So what did I feel? Absolutely nothing.

Growing up as a middle-class 'Brown' boy in Jamaica, with my social and intellectual background (by proxy through my family, not me personally), I felt completely empowered and worthy in every way in relation to anybody in the whole world. So, I didn't think of myself as someone who could be the object of racial abuse, considered inferior just because of my colour. I remember instances, either in training when the banter got personal and heated and I laughed it off (which sometimes irritated the perpetrator), or in matches, when overt racism reared its ugly head, I would laugh it off and my teammates or manager Graham Taylor would be proud of me for 'putting up with it'. They would say, 'Well done' for not letting it get to me, and I'd say, 'It really doesn't bother me' and the response would be, 'Good lad, chin up' and I'd say again, 'IT REALLY DOESN'T BOTHER ME.'

Why couldn't people see that it really didn't bother me? The reason it didn't is because I didn't see how an ignorant person could feel superior to me and seek to subjugate me because of the colour of my skin. I fully understand the history of colonialism and historical racism and the negative effect it had on Black people worldwide in every respect. I understand the emotive ramifications of calling someone 'nigger' and the commonly held theories of Black people's moral and intellectual deficiencies. But history doesn't define who we are now, and language and beliefs of the past which may have been used to disempower Black people, I believe, cannot affect the way in which I see myself today.

I had a great relationship with all of my white teammates and even when racist epithets were thrown around, in jest or otherwise, it was like water off a duck's back to me. I absolutely understand and empathise with any Black player who, at the time, felt degraded or dehumanised by such treatment, who responded violently or otherwise, because I don't know the environment in which they were brought up, or the experiences of racism that had affected their own or their families' lives. But having second-hand knowledge of what life was like for immigrant Black families in the '60s and '70s, it was most likely one of being discriminated against with unequal social and educational opportunities and a life of struggle to be considered worthy. There may have been a lot of potentially excellent Black footballers who were lost to the game, because they wouldn't put up with the 'banter'/abuse that was dished out in the '70s and '80s.

I understand the nature of my personal experience within the game, but what about the broader reality of racism in football?

NATIONAL IDENTITY AND RACE

I made my England debut in 1983, aged 19. When I played for England, sometimes my loyalty and desire were questioned, because I wasn't born in this country. This was a question of national identity, not racism, because other Black players who played for England were never doubted in the same way.

National identity is a much better gauge of one's identity than one's race, because I believe that the cohesiveness and similarity of experiences and cultures will have a bigger impact on the constitution of your identity, than your colour. My response to that issue was that while I wasn't born in England and I became a British citizen through a process of naturalisation (which meant I could play for England, Scotland, Northern

Ireland or Wales), my absolute loyalty lies with the group I have chosen or the group that chose me. That was England. Does that mean, if I were playing against England for any of the other home nation teams, I wouldn't have tried as hard? Absolutely not.

In fact, what normally happens is that in circumstances like mine, where one can play for any of the home nations, England would almost always be the first choice. But if after a while it's apparent that England isn't going to ask you, you would probably choose to play for one of the others. In my case, unusually, England asked first.

Look at John Aldridge or Jason McAteer, they are both English but played for the Republic of Ireland and they both gave 100 per cent, even more against England, yet they weren't born in Ireland. That's because their loyalties lay with the group they had chosen or the group that had chosen them.

Let me go a step further to explain how our loyalty to our chosen group is more important than where we are born or what race we are. I'll use Stuart Pearce as an example. To me, he is the quintessential Englishman who epitomises the British bulldog spirit, the Churchillian 'up and at 'em, over the top' Englishman. I know Stuart and he may or may not admit it, but after his 69 English caps, with the passion and pride he felt getting every one of them, if his 70th international cap was magically (don't ask how) going to be playing for Cameroon against England, he would give 100 per cent. He would be as committed to his team because that would be who he identified with, and who he was loyal to for the 90-minute duration of the game.

PERCEPTIONS OF RACISM: WHITE ON BLACK AND BLACK ON WHITE

I often wonder why white footballers wouldn't feel insulted if they were to be racially abused. I'm not talking about using nationalities such as, 'You Scottish, you French, English, German, Italian so-and-so', I mean if someone was to say, 'You white [insert appropriate term here]!' The reason is because that isn't an insult. There has never been a negative connotation attached to whiteness. So why, if white people are not offended by it, do you expect me to be offended by being called, 'You Black [insert suitable term here]'? Now, I know people will say it's because of the history of slavery and the way Black people were perceived and treated back then as well as now. But I refuse to feel or to be made to feel inferior by words. As Black American civil rights activist Rosa Parks said, 'No one can make you feel inferior without your consent.'

I've spoken in the past about discrimination also going both ways, white on Black, and Black on white. Many have used this argument to say, 'That's just the way it is', so there's no difference. The fundamental difference is that Black on white discrimination can affect individual white people, but it has no effect on the ability of white society in general to maximise its economic, social and educational opportunities, whereas white on Black discrimination can disenfranchise, stifle and hold back entire Black societies.

Of course, as a player you can always walk off the football field in response to overt racial abuse, and pressure can be brought to bear on the perpetrators. But what if the fans decided to incessantly and collectively boo a Black player each time he touched the ball, or ran past a section of the crowd, or took a throw-in, and cheered every time he lost the ball, or was fouled, or beaten to the ball? We would all know the real reason why they were booing or cheering, but nothing could be done about it, because you are allowed to boo. Even if you ban booing, there would still be a way to display racism towards any Black player without it being illegal. You can't make monkey chants at a player, because that's illegal, but when he comes to take a throw, and you catch each other's eye (as can easily happen), you can scratch your armpit in an ape-like fashion, and if questioned, say your armpit was itchy. Both you and the Black player know your intention, but you can't be prosecuted or banned from matches because it's impossible to prove racist intent here.

In many respects the sense of either feeling unworthy, or people trying to make you feel inferior, doesn't come from how the individual in question feels about your Blackness; it stems from the perception of what Black represents. If it didn't, a Black person who is intelligent, handsome, rich, good and possesses any other positive character traits you can think of, would not feel insulted if racially abused. It's the idea of what he represents, not him personally that in his mind is the insulting aspect. If he were to think about his own personal character and achievements, he would laugh at the suggestion that he is inferior.

This is the biggest problem in society: people are being discriminated against, but it can't be proven, so nothing can be done about it. Rather than looking to create laws and sanctions to outlaw it, let's educate people so that they won't even want to do it. Because, as we all know, prevention is better than the cure.

THE MEDIA AND RACISM

When I was twenty years old, I went to South America with the England national team to play against Brazil, Chile and Uruguay. Yes, that was the tour on which I scored 'that goal'. But I'm not telling you about this because of the goal, which was highlighted worldwide, but because of something that happened on the tour which today would have made that goal seem almost a minor and trivial incident.

The far-right, political fascist party, the National Front, or NF, funded three of their supporters to travel with the England team on the same plane. That's how teams travelled back then, on regular commercial airlines. And these NF supporters were allowed to tag along to matches and training sessions with their NF banners in full view. So, there they were, from Heathrow, sitting in the plane, unfurling their banners when we got off the plane in Rio for all to see, draping them over the seats in the Maracana stadium, outside the hotel, at the training sessions. It was a bit embarrassing for the white players and the press who travelled with us, but Mark Chamberlain (father of Liverpool's Alex Oxlade-Chamberlain) and I were told to just ignore them and not to let it get to us, which it didn't. They were being photographed and were treated as normal England supporters and not a lot of fuss was made of them; even in the media, there were only a few lines devoted to this story.

Fast forward ten years from that time when the anti-racism programmes started and the press started to champion the anti-racism cause and report on and highlight each and every racially motivated incident, no matter how small, in the name of 'the media against racism'. I know a lot of the same journalists who were there in 1984 in South America who never said a word, but in 1994 were shouting from the rooftops about racism. Their response to this seeming hypocrisy was, 'Well, that was the way it was back then', which to me means that they considered the issue of racism in sport unimportant in 1984. So why was it important in 1994? Were they not culpable in 1984? What brought about the change ten years later? They were grown men in 1984, and their perceptions and values were already formed, so to me how could they have changed their sensibilities and opinions just a decade later? Were they 'unconsciously racist' in 1984 and not so in 1994? If there hadn't been a drive to get rid of racism in football in 1994, would they have gone along with the status quo? In my opinion, the answer is absolutely! I'm not criticising the journalists who seemed to have changed their opinion ten years later. They're like anyone else: if they are not affected by it, they just go along with it.

In the build-up to the 2018 World Cup, there was a drive to create a negative perception about the anticipated racism in Russia. Every man and his dog was coming out of the woodwork to say how terrible it will be for the Black players and their families in Russia, and that they should walk off the field if they heard any racist chanting or language. I had a heated debate on talkSPORT with a Black journalist, about what Black players should do in that eventuality. In our discussion, I explained that first of all racism understandably exists because of the world's historical view of Blackness, and that we should look at ourselves before coming down on Russia and FIFA. I argued once again about the responsibility we have to look at all aspects and institutions of society, not just Russia, FIFA, John Terry or Luis Suárez. I mentioned the journalist's own industry, and the under-representation of ethnic minorities as an example of unconscious racial bias. He read out the names of four or five Black/ethnic minority journalists who were employed in the mainstream media, as if to suggest there was no problem with 'his' industry.

The conversation then took a ridiculous turn when we began to discuss when a Black player should feel justified to walk off the pitch. Should it be when he hears, or thinks he hears, one idiot shouting a racist remark, or 100 or 1,000 of them? Should it be if the remark he hears is racist, or just general abuse? Should white players walk off if they hear something, even if the Black player doesn't? There would be chaos. What about if the whole stadium clap in a sarcastic way? Meaning, when Black opposition players have the ball, and they are obviously not supporting him. Is that racist abuse? This has always been my argument in the struggle against racism: you can't pass laws to stop racism because there will always be ways of getting around those laws to make your racist views be heard. The solution is to try to make people see why it's wrong to even want to show discrimination in the first place. While I was purposefully giving ridiculous scenarios as to why it would be impossible to stop racist behaviour by leaving it up to the players to decide when they thought they were being abused, we are now being told that as long as we feel abused, even if no one else agrees, we are within our rights to act accordingly. As one person's interpretation of abuse can so greatly differ from another's, the consequence would be that if a Black player is simply getting booed, he can interpret this as racist abuse and is well within his rights to walk off and have the game abandoned.

In order to justify colonialism, Black people for years had been told that they had no backbone, were mentally weak and child-like, and needed white society's management and protection. Now we are being told, 'If you feel upset by the naughty crowd booing you and can't handle it, we'll protect you. Come and cry on our shoulder.' Look, I'm not trivialising or belittling real racism, but we shouldn't interpret every negative incident that happens to Black players as racism. There is general abuse of the opposition in football which will always be there.

In our conversation, the journalist's defence of his own indus-try, however, was interesting because the idea of worthiness and belonging comes from a shared identity, and while he had a shared identity with Black people, he also shared an identity with journalists, so he had empathy with both. However, if you're going to champion anti-racism and call out discrimina-tion where it occurs, you can't wear two hats. I can't go around saying that there was racial abuse in the '80s in football, on the field by players and in the stands by fans, but none at all by my Liverpool/Watford teammates or our own fans towards Black opponents. I either have to deny it happened all together or tell the truth as I see it in its entirety. So, in this context, I couldn't say to the journalist that if he felt that way, i.e. that his industry was less culpable than others, that he was wrong.

However, this is, in my opinion, an example of one of the biggest problems we have when truly tackling the issue. People in the limelight complain when we are either affected by racism or have something to lose and we look to blame others, but we don't look at the industries we are a part of.

Less than six months after this chat, racism in football raised its ugly head once again when Raheem Sterling was racially abused by some fans at Chelsea. He had a very mature assessment of the incident. Among other things, he said that the media fuelled the perception that football fans hold towards Black players. I wished that he had widened the debate to include a discussion about the media's responsibility (or irresponsibility) with respect to the perception of Black people more generally, as I've said all along, but at least it was a start. With this new narrative, lots of people jumped on the bandwagon to point the finger at journalists – 'Now let's add them to the list of the guilty, and we'll soon get to the reality.' But the reality is, it's EVERYONE.

The same journalist got in on the act again: initially he laid the blame solely on radio and television, but he then went on to say, 'The brutal truth, is that other areas of the media are just as guilty', meaning the written press as well. However, he added, 'But not sports journalists as they have a better relationship with Sterling than you think.' In doing so, he absolved his personal working field of any blame, pointing the finger else-where. Haven't we heard that somewhere before? It's not us, it's them? Once again it would be like me saying, it wasn't my teammates or fans, it's only the opposition. I understand why the journalist said this, because had he condemned sports journalism what would his colleagues' reactions be towards him? He is one of 'them' as well as being 'Black'. While, con-versely, he doesn't necessarily have to identify with the 'other' media. It's all about survival. But I say, either put your head above the parapet, or keep it down. There's nothing wrong with either approach, but don't put your head halfway up.

What are we trying to do? Are we trying to stop racism? Or do we just not want to see or hear it? The way we are going about tackling the problem is designed to 'not hear it' at football stadiums, because all the national football associations can do is govern football, which is for 90 minutes twice a week. And all they can do is say to racist football fans, 'Any racist chant-ing or slogans in the ground, you'll be ejected.' Is that threat enough to change the minds of racists, unconscious or not, or would they just have to keep their mouths shut for 90 minutes twice a week? It takes more than that to dismantle 200 years of creating, underpinning and validating the perception of Black people's worth.

BLACK PLAYERS ON BOTH SIDES

I remember playing at West Ham when I was around twenty-one and being racially abused by West Ham fans, then seeing those same fans cheer Bobby Barnes (no relation) when he did something well, and thinking to myself, 'How come they're cheering him and booing me, and we are both Black?' I also heard some Watford fans racially abuse Black players from other teams, but cheer Luther Blissett and myself. I was racially abused by some Liverpool fans when I played for Watford, but later loved by those same fans when I played for Liverpool.

When we think about overt racism in football in the past, and the acceptance and apathy of everyone within society towards it, I'm reminded about an incident that took place at Vicarage Road, where Watford were playing Oldham at home. Watford had a few Black players on the pitch that day, as did Oldham. Towards the end of the first half, a few Watford fans were racially abusing the Oldham players: you could hardly hear it, but it was loud enough for Watford manager Graham Taylor to hear it from the bench. The half-time whistle went and the players trudged down the tunnel into the dressing room to wait for the manager to come in to give the usual half-time team talk, but Graham didn't appear in the dressing room until just before it was time to go out for the second half. The players thought it strange that he wasn't there for around ten minutes. They only found out later what he actually did, which was to go up to where the PA system was being broadcast, grab the microphone, and go out to the middle of the pitch and berate the 'fans' who were abusing the Oldham players, asking them how did they think their OWN Black players must feel having to listen to that abuse, and that if it happened again, the culprits would NEVER be allowed back into Vicarage Road to watch their beloved team. That's the integrity that he had, and the principles he stood for at a time when racism in football wasn't even part of the conversation.

Lots of football teams have Black players, and you may even love them if they're any good. So, you elevate them out of Blackness and abuse the others. But it's not personal.

I've often heard white people say, 'We've been racially abused as well because football fans sing things like, "You Scouse bastard."' You hear insults at football matches towards so many different nationalities, and people complain of racism. England v Scotland matches were notorious for, 'You English [insert appropriate term here]', 'You Scottish [insert suitable term here].' Is that racism? No, but is it worse than racism?

A Juventus footballer called Medhi Benatia once cut short an interview because he claimed he heard a racist comment in his earpiece from someone who called him a 'Moroccan shit'. Is that a racial insult? Can you racially abuse Jewish people? If the Jewish people are a race, what race does a Black Jewish person belong to? Can you change your race? If a Chinese man converts to Judaism, what race is he? Are Iraqi Jews a different race to Iraqi Muslims? From a legal perspective, it will be impossible to come to a conclusion about racist intent in the cases I've just mentioned. The situation which people find the easiest not only to identify, but to do something about, is racism against Black people.

Why at football matches are we able to insult those who are fat, short, ugly, cockneys, Scousers, Mancs, Geordies, bald etc. – the list can go on and on – and the recipients of those insults are in no way bothered about it enough to walk off the field or let it affect them? But being called 'Black [insert suitable term here]' is so offensive, that the 'poor, weak Black man' can't take the abuse which isn't real or personal.

When I first went to Liverpool, I met a Black guy who said he supported Liverpool but had never been to a game. When I asked him why, he said he would never go to Anfield until they signed an 'average Black player'. That struck me as strange until I thought about the meaning behind his statement. Remember this was in 1987, a different time to now; what he meant by this was that Liverpool and other top English clubs signed many average white players, without their race coming into question, but any Black player going to any top English club would be judged by his ability as a 'Black' player to be up to the highest standard for the task. This guy felt that inequality in football would be over (on the field at least) when Liverpool signed a crap Black player, like they have signed a lot of crap white players without their crappiness being linked to their colour. This way of thinking can be extrapolated to many other industries where Black people have to be better than their white counterparts to be considered to have the same worth as an employee.

At the 2018 Chelsea v Spurs Carabao Cup semi-final match at Wembley, three men were charged with racially aggravated offences. This, like other recent incidents, surprised a lot of people who thought those days were over. They were never over, they just were not reported: now they are. But once again, we have to be careful about what we consider to be racially aggravated abuse, as opposed to abuse of a player who happens to be Black. The latter is left to any individual's interpretation, which in turn can be influenced by the new directive of zero tolerance over comments like 'lazy' or 'thick'.

So, who decides whether there is racism attached to the inclusion of these words when describing the performance of a Black player? While we may say that in the public arena, words like 'thick' and 'lazy' shouldn't be used to describe Black players, or else journalists may be sacked, in the rest of the country, on training fields, can coaches call Black players 'lazy' or 'stupid', or will Black players be able to get them fired for racial discrimination? In my opinion, the people coming up with these ideas haven't got a clue as to the solution to the real problem.

In the '70s and early '80s, negative traits of Black players were based on the incorrect perception of their unreliability, irresponsibility, attitude, commitment, etc. Those myths have now been dispelled. These days the perception is about their ostentatiousness, the cars they drive, the way they dress, flaunting their wealth. So, Raheem Sterling was 100 per cent right when he used the comparison between two young players at Manchester City, one Black and one white. While the white one was portrayed as responsible and dutiful for buying his mother a house for two million pounds. The Black one was portrayed as financially irresponsible and flashy for buying his mother a house for a similar price.

Surely, our Black forefathers didn't go through what they did, for me to now be so weak minded and fragile as to feel insulted by every little thing that I come up against? Raheem was rightly seen to be laughing at the men abusing him at Stamford Bridge, and he wasn't bothered by it in the slightest, because as he aptly said it didn't surprise him. But in the days following the incident the world rallied round in support of 'poor Raheem', as if it affected him so much that he needed our support.

This happened to me as well, when an Ian Wright programme was aired that depicted how difficult it was for Black footballers in the '80s and showed me being interviewed about my time at Liverpool when racism was rife within football. It never affected me or had a negative impact on my life or career, but the sympathy I received after was incredible. At an event I attended soon after the programme was shown, I received a standing ovation by people there who had seen the interview and felt sympathy for what I had gone through in my football career. Let me say, while I have empathy with any Black person who feels the need for sympathy, help or support for their experiences and would never judge them, I've never felt the need for the type of reception I got that night. It seems to me that Raheem might feel the same way.

As I mentioned at the start of the book, I used to think racial abuse didn't bother me because I felt just as worthy as any white football fan who abused me and therefore, they couldn't affect me. But, as I've got older and thought more about racial discourse, I've come to realise that actually I didn't just feel worthy or equal, I felt MORE worthy and superior to those idiots who abused me. And it wasn't because they were idiots, it was because of the fact that I was an educated, middle-class person from an elite family in society in Jamaica. My race never hampered me personally in any way, shape or form in my opinion, but the age-old class/elite structure that framed my life from an early age was apparent in an unconscious way. My feelings had nothing to do with wealth, as my family were never super wealthy but due to my father's position in the military's upper echelons, they had a status which afforded us a certain class privilege. This, in my own mind, which is a testament to the power of class, superseded society's perception of race. It can, therefore, be just as problematic in terms of discrimination between classes.

An interesting concept when thinking of acts of racism in football was demonstrated recently when Marcus Rashford received racist abuse on social media after Manchester United's loss to Villarreal in a Europa League game in 2021. We are told that the reason for this is because he is Black. Here is another example of how we are trying to oversimplify a very complex and nuanced topic. He missed a couple of chances that could have led to Manchester United winning the Europa League, so the abuse ensued, but had he scored those chances, he wouldn't have received any racist abuse at all. Does that mean that the people who racially abused him are only racially biased when he misses an open goal?

If we no longer hear or see any racist acts in football stadiums or on social media, that doesn't mean it no longer exists. Just because someone doesn't say something out loud (for fear of being punished) it doesn't mean they don't still believe it. If that was the case, then the easiest way to overcome racism would be for Black players to never miss open goals. We wouldn't hear any racist abuse then; we could feel that we have defeated racism. What a ridiculous way to think!

Another example: Bright Osayi-Samuel, then at QPR, gets racially abused in December 2020 for missing a chance to win a game against Norwich, despite scoring a penalty prior to this. If he scored the goal then he could be a hero to the same people who would abuse him, he could become 'elevated out of Blackness' to be accepted. But, because he missed, he's kept where the general perception of Black people is . . . below the average person and unworthy. So, should we strive for that acceptance towards our successful Black heroes, or try to change the PERCEPTION of our unsuccessful average Black people?

When we hear about football fans racially abusing Black players, often the other fans of that club will say, 'Well, those people aren't real fans.' That's bullshit. Why aren't they real fans? Because real fans can't be racially biased? Do we hear milkmen, postmen, doctors, lawyers or people from any other occupation say, if one of their group gets caught making a racist comment that they are then not a real milkman, postman, doctor or lawyer? As if you can't be racially biased if you are a real football fan? In fact, at times the opposite is true. It seems you can't be a real fan of (insert any club here) if you appreciate or like ANY player from another club, never mind a Black player from another club. So, your true loyalty is hatred towards every other rival club and player, and if he happens to be Black, then how do you show your hatred? In the way society has taught you for hundreds of years! If that player isn't Black, you will use more general stereotypical, conditioned abuse such as, 'robbing scouser', 'northern thicko', 'ginger so-and-so', 'southern softie' or any other lies you have learnt about those different groups through indoctrination throughout your life.

TRANSACTIONAL BENEFIT

The issue of stereotyping is not just a feature of association football, though gradual transformative measures are in evidence in other sports. In American football these days, things do seem to be changing in that there are more Black quarterbacks (which is traditionally known as a 'thinking' position) than in the past. This is because of the transactional benefit of having an athletic QB who can run as well as throw to the team. However, I wonder whether there will start to be Black QBs who aren't necessarily as athletic in terms of speed, whereby using his brain to decide the play is the only quality by which he will be judged, as often is the case for white QBs?

When Jackie Robinson became the first Black player in Major League baseball in the '40s, the obvious transactional benefit was that he could hit home runs; in boxing, Mike Tyson could knock his opponent out, and Usain Bolt could beat the field most times in the 100-metre sprint. All of this can be measured from a financial perspective in terms of attracting sponsorship, the transactional benefit to those institutions is obvious and tangible, and we can accept the participation of Black sportsmen and women. But when it comes to management or leadership, there has to be a belief that there can be a transactional benefit BEFORE it is proven or measured, and that's where it becomes difficult for Black men and women and other disenfranchised groups if they aren't successful straight away.

The transactional benefit of inclusivity on the sports field for Black athletes was the reason we were allowed access to our chosen sport by stakeholders. However, they do not see any transactional benefit to allowing us into the higher echelons of major industries at administration, leadership or management levels, as there is still a negative perception of our intellectual and moral equality.

IS FOOTBALL THE PROBLEM?

I've said all along that the solution to racial bias in any industry is to tackle it in mainstream society first, then the industry will fall into line. But let's talk about football again.

As I'm writing this book, new incidents are popping up almost weekly of racial abuse towards players, so can we really say that things are getting better since this anti-racism campaign in football started nearly thirty years ago? No! And it won't, as long as we approach it in the same way that we always have: with fines, banning, and walking off the field.

In 2013, we remember Kevin-Prince Boateng walking off the field during an AC Milan match after several players suffered racial abuse from a section of the crowd, and being told, 'That's what needs to be done'. There have been countless such incidents, a recent one being Sulley Muntari walking off the field in Italy in 2017, subsequently being banned, and a call for all players to strike in support of him. Once again, to many this looks like a millionaire footballer calling for empathy for himself because his voice can be heard, and others jumping on the bandwagon.

Here is the problem: we live in an unfair, racially biased society, which will allow and encourage a few people from discriminated groups to be 'elevated' out of their groups and be accepted in the 'dominant' group. That privilege isn't there for everyone, and if we tell the 'average' people of the disenfranchised group that the way to get what you want, like Sulley Muntari, is to walk off their equivalent of 'the field', you're setting them up for disaster. It's fine that to prove there is equality in football and that the authorities are doing something about the situation, Sulley's ban has been reversed, and he may even win an award for standing up against racism. But do we really believe that some voiceless Black bus driver, traffic warden, unskilled worker, part-time worker can do the same thing with the same outcome, without proof of discrimination? Absolutely not.

And here is the biggest problem: football is an easy target, because of the overt racism which is there for all to see. Ninety-nine per cent of what some people know is racial bias, can't be proven. So those people who are very obviously discriminated against such as women, members of the LGBTQ community, disabled people, unlike footballers who are told to, 'walk off the field', can't 'walk off the field of life' and get any justice or reward. So, stop telling people this is what they have to do!

I have spoken about the fact that the most distinguished and intelligent people of yesteryear believed Black people were inferior, and how so much literature, film and propaganda endorsed and reinforced that view. So, what chance do we have as people of average intelligence, even people who believed in and fought for equality for themselves, but not necessarily for other people who they considered inferior?

When the 2018 World Cup came around, we were all so excited about the new, young England team. What concerned me, was the narrative surrounding this new, 'diverse' England team that the country could get behind because now it consisted of different cultures and races. For the last thirty-five years there have been several Black players in the squad, and I remember an England game at least ten years ago when there were at least seven Black players on the pitch representing England at the same time. It's as if we are trying to forget those 'bad old days' when Black players were abused, and instead, convince people that this is a new era where Black players are now just getting into the England team. I found that very insulting to generations of Black players of the past. Are we wiping them out of the positive history of England football teams by suggesting that Raheem Sterling, Kyle Walker, Dele Ali, Jesse Lingard are more important than Viv Anderson, Laurie Cunningham, Cyrille Regis or Luther Blissett were in changing perceptions of Black footballers? It's true that they are playing at a time when society's acceptance of England's Black players may have changed; but I find it disrespectful that those past heroes are forgotten by spinning this new diverse England team mantra as if they are the pioneers of Black participation in English football.

An interesting opinion came from my friend Dutch footballer and manager Ruud Gullit. He correctly (in my opinion) said that the problem is not just in football but in all walks of society, and that the debate should be led by people who have come across racism, who understand the problem better than white middle-class men, and have a better understanding of the solution. Where I disagreed with him though was when he said that he, or people like him, can't do it because he is 'privileged'. I firmly believe that it's PEOPLE LIKE US, me included, members of the privileged Black society who must speak up for the less privileged, because they DON'T HAVE A VOICE. And I don't mean speak out in support of Raheem Sterling, John Barnes, Idris Elba, famous Black singers, actors, and so on; I mean speak out for the wider community.

We, as Black people, know which form of bias needs to be focused on first, but what do we think is more urgent in this fight to tackle racism: stopping a few Bulgarian fans racially abusing Black football players and stopping commentators calling Black players lazy? Or tackling racial inequality and injustice in our communities, aiming to strive for equal opportunities for everyone with regard to education, jobs and standards of living? It doesn't make sense to me the sheer disproportionate amount of energy that can be put into high-lighting and criticising one person, e.g. the thirteen-year-old football fan who shouted racist abuse to Tottenham player Son Heung-min, something he has learnt from what he has seen all his life growing up in this society. Should we not be asking, why was he compelled to act in this way, and who and what has taught him that this is acceptable? The answer is the environment and society that he has grown up in, and that includes a lot more than just a football stadium. Again, sadly it is quicker and easier to point at and blame one person than to look at the bigger picture.

Liverpool's Jordan Henderson stated he felt that white players should also be speaking out against racism alongside their Black colleagues and he's absolutely right. In fact, they should be speaking out even more so than Black players. Coming from a white person it won't then be seen as, 'Black players just having a chip on their shoulder' or 'complaining and playing the race card'. Jordan made an interesting point in saying, 'Racism is like an assault with words', however I think that verbal racist abuse is actually the least destructive or impactful dynamic of racism. It is the structural, insidious, systemic, unseen and unheard racism that is more impactful and that we need to eradicate first.

2

'THE PROBLEM WITH BLACK MANAGERS IS . . .'

This book isn't about how terrible it is for me, or for football, that there are no or very few Black managers. For this is only a microcosm of the problem of racial bias. Having said that, there is one particular incident that stands out for me. It involves a very famous ex-footballer manager who I know well and like a lot, so he won't be mentioned by name. In no way am I accusing him of being racist, but he is probably exactly like you and me: unconsciously racially biased. Anyway, we were having a conversation about the lack of Black managers in the game.

'There aren't any good ones,' he said. 'The problem with Black managers is . . .' Same old story.

'They don't get qualified, network, apply for jobs,' he went on. Same old stereotype.

I was staring at him as he uttered these sentiments, and then it suddenly dawned on him: I WAS BLACK! Then it suddenly dawned on me: HE DIDN'T SEE ME AS BLACK!

I'd heard this before, but never experienced it without words. I know it suddenly dawned on him because his facial expression and body language displayed a sense of embarrassment, and an overcompensation on his part by bringing someone else into the conversation and saying in a manner of jest, 'I was just saying to Barnesy that there weren't any good Black managers', while winking and pointing in my direction as if he knew I was or could be one and was only taking the piss. I could easily have pulled him up on it but understand that this is the way the world is and there is a reason for it. So, rather than winning little battles of putting people down or feeling powerful by making people afraid, I suggest, let's focus on the bigger picture.

I was fortunate to play football in the era I did, because despite there being racism towards Black players, I was still able to fulfil my potential and dreams. At that time, racism couldn't stop the physical capabilities of any Black sportsman, like it did ten or twenty years earlier when the negative perception of Black footballers meant their actual ability was questioned. I was, however, unfortunate in the timing of wanting to be a football manager, because of the continued negative perception of Black players' leadership ability to be good managers. Today, just as in previous decades, when the odd, successful Black player would be held up to convince people progress was being made, there are a few Black managers, like Frank Rijkaard, Ruud Gullit and Chris Hughton, who will, no doubt, be held up to prove there is no racial bias in football management.

When the first Black football manager, Tony Collins, managed Rochdale from 1960–67 and took them to their only major final, the Football League Cup, with a 36 per cent win record, it's surprising to hear that he lasted that long being a Black man. Why, you may ask? The question as to whether Black men could be good managers wasn't an issue back then: he was the only one. But as more Black candidates became available and the status quo became more threatened, those negative racial-stereotype perceptions crept in to stop Black people getting such jobs. This has always happened: society doesn't mind one or two, but has to step in when numbers of minorities begin to threaten the majority.

I hear the question a lot particularly from the media: 'Can Black players make good coaches?' That is an overtly racist question, although it comes from an unconsciously racist place. The very question pre-supposes that there is a possibility, no matter how slim, that a person may not be a good manager because of the colour of his or her skin. You might as well ask, 'Can a woman be a CEO of a company?' Isn't that a sexist question? Absolutely!

There haven't been many Black managers in the game of football, and once again this isn't due to a personal perception of any individual Black manager's abilities, but to a perception of Black people generally, and their ability to lead. You look at a country like Brazil where Black players have played a leading role on the field for close to one hundred years. From the so-called inventor of the overhead kick, Leônidas, in the 1920s, to Pelé, Didi, Vavá and Garrincha, in the 1950s. Up to this day there aren't many, if any, Black coaches (now please don't find one or two and then trash my argument because 'there is one, so ha!'). Why is that? I've heard from many of my white contemporaries that Black players don't want to get qualified, go through the ranks, go on courses, network, etc.

Similar to the argument that there is a perception that women and LGBTQ members are discriminated against; in the last ten years or so in the English Premier League there is arguably a group of football managers who are being discriminated against, and they are . . . white. WHITE ENGLISH MANAGERS, can you believe it? If you speak to Sam Allardyce, Alan Pardew, Harry Redknapp, etc., they will tell you English managers aren't and won't be given a chance at the top five or six Premier League clubs if those jobs become available. I also know that to be true, so if even white English managers aren't being given top jobs, why is it so hard to believe that a Black manager's chances are significantly lower? White English managers are being denied the chance to manage top clubs not because they are 'white', but because they're 'English'.

This, once again, comes down to the perception of a certain group of people's ability to be top managers. So, like any form of discrimination, it's not personal to the individual. So, like any form of discrimination, it's not personal to the individual. When you can see examples of what people just like you have achieved, and realise that there are opportunities and pathways for you to be successful, it's easier to be motivated, hungry and inspired. If you suffer a setback, and life hasn't shown you that it's because of the colour of your skin, it's easier to become more determined, to try harder and be more committed and focused than before, because you know you can make it. Conversely, when life has shown you that it's much more difficult for people like you to achieve what you want, then it's a setback. When there are little or no examples of success for you to aspire to, it's easy to become demotivated and unsure of yourself. Why not? You are constantly being told that we are all equal; you are being told that we all have the same opportunities, but *you* have failed, and the majority of people like you have also done so. Of course, you begin to question yourself.

Football goes through trends. When Gérard Houllier came to Liverpool and was successful, French coaches were *de rigueur*. When Rafa Benítez was successful at Liverpool, the fad was for Spanish coaches. They say it needs a successful Black coach for Black managers to be given more opportunities, but I doubt this, because Frank Rijkaard won the Champions League with Barcelona, yet that didn't open the door to a host of Black managers. If a Black coach is successful, it doesn't mean all Black coaches will be successful; similarly, if a Black coach is unsuccessful, it shouldn't mean that all Black coaches will be unsuccessful yet unfortunately that seems to be the mode of thought.

When we talk about being given an opportunity, what do we mean? While many people might think that football is one of the most racially biased industries in the world and football fans are among some of the most racist people in the world, I absolutely disagree. Football fans are members of society first then members of the football fraternity second, and as such, they are influenced by the environment in which they live. Their ideals, perceptions, values and principles are formed by the society in which they live, and they carry those attitudes with them to the football arena. So, if they are racist, they are racist members of society who happen to be football fans, not the other way around. So, if we want to get rid of racism in football, we have to get rid of it in society first.

I had a conversation with an intelligent man about the Black managers debate and the reason there are so few. He said that it has nothing to do with colour, that culturally the best managers are European and South American. Of course, he didn't mean what he said to come across in the way it did, but unconsciously when talking about who he thought were culturally better managers he did mean 'white' without even thinking about it. I pointed out that myself and all the other Black potential managers here and in France are European, and that lots of the Black Brazilian ex-players who want to be coaches are South American.

Football is one of the most homogenous, passionate and inclusive phenomenon of all time. It creates an identity like no other, among fans of the same club, and football fans generally. So, if anyone, no matter his colour, sexual orientation, religion is going to come to your club and make it successful, you will accept him. Any Black or homosexual or Muslim manager, at any club, if he is successful, will be supported and loved by all the fans. The problem, I believe, is when they are unsuccessful; then our unconscious bias and the perceptions we hold about the ability of the group in which that person belongs to in being a successful manager comes to the fore much quicker than it would if it were a straight white man who was equally as unsuccessful. Based on that individual's failure, we ask ourselves can a Black/ homosexual/Muslim manager really do the job? Being given the job is not the end of being given a chance. Being given a chance is, yes, firstly being given a job, but more importantly it also encompasses being given the trust, and having the initial respect from fans, players and our bosses, that they 100 per cent believe in your ability.

Rather than coming across as arrogant and saying, 'Black managers can be as good as any white manager,' I always say, 'Black managers should be given the chance to be as bad as white managers.' What I mean by that statement is, how many 'bad' white managers have we seen fail, and are given second, third, even fourth and fifth jobs after that? The majority of 'bad' Black managers get one job, and never get a second chance.

There have been, and this includes me, Black players who have been given 'jobs', not real 'opportunities' to be managers, but they haven't been given the same amount of time to fail as their white counterparts. By that I mean that Black managers, who have not started off well in a particular season, have been sacked much more quickly than their white counterparts with similar records.

MANAGING CELTIC FC

My first job in football management was at Celtic in 1999. Race didn't play a part in my failure there to any degree, nor did my 'Englishness'. The fact that I didn't have a history there may have been a slight factor, but the fact that I was a novice and arguably hadn't earned the right to be there played a larger role.

The most interesting thing about my time at Celtic, are the actual 'facts' about my tenure. From the first week there was a press agenda against me revolving around my 'worthiness' (not racial I may add) to be there, and every decision was being questioned even when we won. While we were winning this didn't affect the players, but I knew that if we went through a sticky patch this could be problematic, as I thought if these problems arose even while we were winning, what chance did I have if we started to lose? The worst thing about my time at Celtic was the media's portrayal of me as arrogant and aloof. I believe the most important quality any human being can have is humility, and I would rather be the worst manager in history but be humble than a successful and arrogant manager.

As with anything in life, we are greatly influenced by the media, so some Celtic fans obviously assumed that the media's perception of me was correct and didn't take to me from the beginning. One of the most important, if not THE most important thing that contributes to success, is the harmony of the group. The club's harmony was being eroded by mainly outside influences, but also by some quarters within the club.

We started off well, with a 5–0 win away at Aberdeen in 1999, and we were doing okay, five or six points behind Rangers who were unbeaten. We won around eleven, drew one and lost two or thereabouts, before Henrik Larsson broke his leg in November; then our captain and most influential player along-side Henrik, Paul Lambert broke his jaw against Rangers at Ibrox the weekend after. We had a Christmas break and came back in January, I won manager of the month, then was sacked in February after losing a cup replay at home to Inverness Caledonian Thistle. This provided the press with what should have been an award-winning headline, 'Super Cally Go Ballistic . . . Celtic Are Atrocious.'

There are, as Rafa Benítez puts it, the 'facts' about my time at Celtic. After Jock Stein, I had the largest percentage of wins than any other first time manager at Celtic. I had a better win percentage than Wim Jansen who won the title at Celtic two years earlier. Martin O'Neil and then Neil Lennon had better win percentages than me, although in Neil's case, Rangers weren't around to challenge them regularly. So, in the history of Celtic managers, as far as win percentage goes, I'm either the fourth or fifth best manager, but my tenure there is still considered a disastrous spell. So much for perceptions and reality.

RACIAL BIAS IN CARIBBEAN AND AFRICAN FOOTBALL

For me, the role of Jamaica's national team manager came seven years later, and not for the want of trying to get back into management at any level in the intervening years. From a footballing perspective, this was not only the most successful period of my career, but the most personally rewarding. As a coach, if you hold certain beliefs and traditions and these come to a positive fruition, then that gives you a sense of self-belief – that you can be successful without necessarily having the best players. If you put in place a philosophy of hard work, commitment, belief and determination and this works, it is immensely satisfying.

We didn't have our best players available for the majority of the time; I used local players, as our better players were mainly at their clubs abroad and wouldn't be released for many of our matches. But we were unbeaten for all of the eleven games in which I was manager, winning seven and drawing four. My stint as manager of this team provided me with first-hand experience of an interesting dynamic. I'd seen previously and now experienced the way that the developing football nations' administrations, as well as their fans and players, responded to their local coaches, and the way they treated and responded to the foreign coaches they employed. I was a Jamaican yet still viewed as a foreign coach, and I believed that worked in my favour. Would they have had the same belief in me had I stayed, been brought up in and lived my whole life in Jamaica? Probably not, as we have seen throughout Caribbean and African football for many years.

When we talk about racial bias, it's not just white people seeing Black people as inferior; it's also some Black people seeing others of their own race as inferior. This is the result of what we also have been wrongly told about ourselves. You may have noticed that I didn't say Blacks seeing themselves as inferior. That's because in Africa, just like in Jamaica, the captains of industry and business and political leaders, through their environment and the education they have received (which is generally a Western one) have been shown the racial hierarchy of the world, and know 100 per cent that they themselves are as equal and worthy as their white counterparts worldwide. However, they don't feel the same about people like them who have been disenfranchised and undereducated due to the circumstances of their birth.

Let's take football in Africa as an example. When a position to coach one of the African teams becomes available, not only are white European coaches given more opportunities to obtain these jobs; the respect, belief and salaries they are given far outweigh those of the local coaches. This is evidence of how all-encompassing racial bias has become, where even majority Black countries discriminate against their own countrymen. You could argue that it has to do with class rather than race, but I disagree. While the middle-class Black leaders may look down on the working-class Black people who they feel are inferior to them and therefore treat accordingly, the white coaches they employ from Europe would oftentimes also be viewed as working-class, undereducated people within their own countries and therefore the European equivalent of those local Black coaches in terms of class. However, what differentiates them from their African counterparts is they're white, so in Africa they are treated with more respect.

Once again, we can't blame the leaders of these developing countries. We have to look at the society in which we/they live, and the impact that modern (relatively speaking) education worldwide has had on the way we view the world around us. Once we are aware of this negative impact, we can then try to change our view and attitudes on this issue.

When I took the Tranmere Rovers job in 2009, I knew it was going to be difficult: the wage bill was reduced to just under a million pounds for the whole squad, so we lost our best three or four players. Nevertheless, I was happy to take the position just to get into management, even under those circumstances. I hear managers talk about waiting for the 'right' opportunity to come along and not to just take 'any' job. For most Black managers unfortunately, that's one luxury we don't have, so if we want to manage, we have to take 'any' job most of the time. It didn't go well, and some Tranmere Rovers fans misunderstood when I said racism played a part in me losing my job as quickly as I did. They thought I was calling them racist. As I've tried to explain all along, it wasn't personal against me. Every Tranmere Rovers fan wanted me to do well and supported me 100 per cent, but when things didn't go well, it was the unconscious negative perception that the fans had of the group of people (of which I belong to), not necessarily of me as an individual, with respect to our capabilities to manage. This is just like the unconscious negative perception Premier League fans of the top English clubs would have of white English managers if things didn't go well at their clubs.

Interestingly, there have been a few high-profile Black managers in the Premier League, but the white English managers should have seen the writing on the wall, when Ruud Gullit and Jean Tigana were appointed at top-level clubs. We, in England, are a contradictory lot. Great Britain came about because of our superiority complex. There was a time when you could just conquer someone else by force, no questions asked. The football hooliganism of the '70s and '80s is a testament to this, as we ran amok throughout Europe, 'conquering' other clubs. But in this day and age, we have a distinct inferiority complex about ourselves; maybe speaking only one language does that. In the old days, you didn't need to speak any other language; nowadays Europeans seem to be more intelligent than we are, because they speak many languages. The major difference between Gullit and Tigana being given management jobs, whereas Blissett, Regis and other Black former players were not being given similar opportunities, was, I believe that the former were seen as 'foreign', so therefore the perception and misconception of them is that they are more intelligent. This is now happening to white English managers in the Premier League.

I recall a programme on television in which Ron Noades, the former Crystal Palace owner in the late '70s, spoke about his team. Back then Palace were considered early pioneers in having a number of Black players, and Noades says how he thought they were suited to certain positions, mainly attacking or out wide, rather than what would have been considered the 'thinking' positions like centre-back or defensive midfield. To be fair to Noades, his thoughts were very much that of the footballing fraternity in general at the time. Years later, I had a conversation with a white colleague of mine about a team with seven Black players, and how successful, disciplined and intelligent the team were, to which he added, 'Yes, but their captain and leader was white.' When I countered his statement by mentioning the successful South Africa team under Black captain Lucas Radebe, he pointed out that he had a white centre-back partner to help hold things together, the clear inference being that they still needed a white presence to be successful as a team.

THE CLASS ISSUE IN FOOTBALL MANAGEMENT

To give you an idea of the nuances and complexities involved in the debate on race and class, and how at times race supersedes class and vice versa, football is a good example. Nowadays, from a playing perspective, race and class play no part (unlike the '70s and '80s when the perception of a Black player's worth and value in certain positions was questioned, as seen above). From the managerial perspective race still plays a huge part in the perception of Black managers. This is with regard to their ability to lead, manage and organise. So, you would expect that because of the disenfranchisement and negative perception of working-class people (even white ones), class would have a negative effect on those white working-class ex-players trying to become managers in a similar way. But in fact, the opposite is true. From Bill Shankly to Alex Ferguson, Kenny Dalglish to Bobby Robson, these are all working-class men who were considered, even before they were successful, to be the right kind of men for the job of a football manager. They were brought up tough, faced adversity, had to fight for everything they achieved; this is the same for Black ex-footballers. So why the different expectations? Even today, take Wayne Rooney or Joey Barton: publicly they were never considered to be the most intelligent people, which of course is wrong, but their ability to manage is never in question because of their working-class background. This is clearly an example of race negatively superseding class.

The plight of Black football managers as opposed to white football managers is similar to the plight of Black working-class people compared to their white counterparts. It's a difficult enough job for white football managers as it stands, but if a white manager fails, it will be because of the perception of him personally, not the perception or question of whether white managers in general are good enough. A Black manager will always have the question of himself personally being good enough and the ability of Black men in general, so it's therefore twice as difficult. This, however, only comes into question in times of failure. If a Black manager is successful, people will attribute that success to him personally, while the issue of whether Black men in general can be successful will still be questioned.

The fact that Tottenham saw fit to give Ryan Mason the job of interim head coach means that an elite organisation trusted him and felt he could do a good job. The fact that it didn't work out very successfully however, hasn't hampered the feeling that he could still do a good job elsewhere. I'm sure he could easily now, because of the trust Tottenham put in him, get a job lower down the leagues. It is the same scenario regarding Ledley King or Chris Powell (two Black assistant coaches who were ahead of Ryan regarding first team affairs). Yes, they were trusted by Tottenham to take over after Mourinho, but now failing would have massively hampered their opportunity for future employment, even at lesser clubs, because the general feeling would have been, 'they had an opportunity and they failed'. All unconscious thoughts by employees and fans alike.

But what about the institutions where prejudice and discrimination hold sway? Is it the system with which the fault lies?

3

IS FOOTBALL INSTITUTIONALLY RACIST?

'No Black person achieved anything alone in the West, the system allowed them to do so. It may seem like a harsh state-ment, but no matter how good they are the system always has the final word on whether they will be allowed into the club.'

James Baldwin, American novelist and activist

When it comes to institutions, we talk for example about the police being institutionally racist, but that statement doesn't truly make sense. For an institution has no power alone: it's the PEOPLE that give it power. As is the case with football, people bring their ideals and values into the institutions they enter. Before you become a member of the police force, you are a member of society. Before you become a member of the football fan fraternity, you are a member of society. Before you become a card-carrying member of any industry, you are a member of society and, as such, you carry your sensibilities with you. You may then argue why is this nasty overt form of racism more prevalent in the police and in football?

This is because of the nature and dynamics of those two institutions. If we address football first, this is a pastime that brings large groups of people into a confrontational situation where abuse and hostility towards the opposition is accepted, indeed expected, so hurling insults is the norm. So how can football fans 'get one over' on the opposition (players and fans) in terms of insults, to let them know that they are inferior? Bearing in mind that football fans were, and still are to a large extent, straight white men? Who has society shown us are inferior to these fans? Black people and ethnic minorities. So, combine this general feeling of unconscious superiority, this accepted forum for aggression and abuse, our wanting to show the opposition that you and your team are better than they are, even though you may be losing to an all-Black team. How do you try to demoralise and disempower the opposition? Tap into what society has shown you to be the inferior group. And the easiest way to do that? Racial abuse.

With regard to the police, as I've said before, we all are unconsciously racially biased, and some unconsciously racially biased members of society choose to go into the police force and some consciously racially biased members of society do too; they also go into every avenue of society as well. They are in an employment sphere which requires them to exert authority and exercise judgement over people, and as such, are called upon every day to make judgement calls as to who is guilty, who is suspect, who is bad, who is a criminal. They then have to enforce their power over these people. How easy is this? What, and who, has society shown them, long before they even think about going into the police force, are typically the 'bad' people? So, when you have a judgement call to make on who to stop and who to arrest, who looks suspicious? Too easy!

To my mind, the police force and the football fraternity aren't institutionally racist; they aren't even unconsciously racist. It's the people in them who are.

In other industries, there aren't such overt forms of racism seen, so surely, it is said, that proves that racism is mainly a problem with the police and football? Not so. In the vast majority of industries, the environment is non-confrontational and aggression towards co-workers is not common, there's no reason to insult or verbally attack an 'opposition'; on the contrary, people are expected to work harmoniously and cooperatively with each other.

You will find that people from all walks of life, when they are in their usual home, work and family environments, are rational, quiet, respectful people; but when they go to a football match, tribalism takes over and they are swept along with whatever is happening at the time. Most would never dream of shouting any kind of abuse, racist or otherwise, at any other time or behave this way walking down the street alone on a Tuesday afternoon at 4 o'clock. But at 3 o'clock on a Saturday and in the company of their fellow supporters, they go along with it. It's not football's fault, it's the people's fault.

Football can do nothing about getting rid of racism, until we get rid of racism in society generally. It will exist in all walks of society, of which football and the police are but a few examples. So, don't blame the police force or football. Better to try to change the society that created and continues to endorse that way of thinking.

Society influences the structures that create institutions, then institutions simultaneously keep society in check to maintain the status quo. Society goes on to blame institutions for inequality and vice versa. So, overall, nothing changes because neither takes responsibility, despite the fact the truth is they are actually one and the same thing. Until they both acknowledge culpability nothing will change, and they'll forever just point the finger and blame each other, leaving people free from having personal responsibility. Certain individuals then may try to get themselves entrenched in those institutions, purporting to want to change them from the inside. They will just continue the finger pointing at society to maintain this vicious circle of no progress in wider society, but they may be able to make tangible change for themselves personally.

POLICE STOP AND SEARCH

The stop and search demographic by the police is very interesting. Young, smart, Black men in BMWs are getting stopped because of the unconscious perception of them as being criminals. This doesn't happen to young, white men in smart cars. From what I can see, poor Black people in beat up cars aren't being stopped by police, but poor white people in beat up cars are. Why? It's because of the perception that the only way a Black man could have enough money in this environment to buy a nice car (if he isn't a footballer, actor or musician) is if he is a criminal, showing off his wealth by buying nice things. Whereas the opportunities for white people to be able to afford nice cars are limitless. That dynamic is quite telling, subliminally, about the way our thought process works. Black people in beat up cars don't get stopped, as that's the kind of car that most of us are expected to drive. There are of course nuances to the debate: the police may stop a young white man driving a nice car in a run-down inner-city area, and this is where class plays a part in perceptions as well, but had he been in a middle-class area they wouldn't have been suspicious as being a white man he would appear to fit in to this kind of environment.

Just like the perception that the young, wealthy, Black foot-baller who buys his mother a house is being 'boastful' with his money. Compared to a young, wealthy, white footballer buying his mother a house being perceived to be dutiful and sensible. A white man driving a cheap car must be a drug dealer; a Black man driving a cheap car isn't because if he had money from drugs, he'd get a nicer car in order to brag.

Pitting disenfranchised people against each other has been the policy for thousands of years. So, in my opinion, Black people now hate Romanians and other Eastern Europeans because we are told they are the problem when it comes to racism in football. They now hate us because we are telling them they are the problem. All while the real enemy of racial equality continues to grow stronger with their handful of collaborators who they have plucked from these disadvantaged groups as 'representatives', who gain more individual power and wealth for themselves.

We wrongly assume that racism towards Black people is worse in Eastern European countries just because of the episodes we see of overt racism at football matches. However, the racism there, where there is a much smaller population of Black people by percentage, isn't necessarily worse. One of the things racism stems from is fear and the feeling of your livelihood being threatened by people who are different to you taking what is considered to be your rightful place and the benefits society gives you. As there is such a small number of Black people in these Eastern European countries, there is not the manpower to impact on the privilege of an individual Eastern European person. However, the systemic racism that we see in Western countries, where there are much larger Black communities, is felt much more because of the perceived threat to the Western Europeans' privileges. Racism against other ethnic minorities (non-Black) in Eastern European countries is much worse though, because the larger numbers of 'others' is seen as more of a threat than that from Black people to the status quo.

From elite white celebrities doing what some people think Black celebrities should be allowed to do, to Black celebrities/ elites doing what the 'firm' or 'establishment' allows them to do on their behalf (which really only serves the ambitions of those elite few) – it's an ongoing debate as the best way to achieve racial equality. Society, the firm or the establishment policy-makers have always been not only the drivers, but the judge and jury of what the right way is and always will be. They only give the illusion that others are making these decisions.

For the last 500 years 'might was right', so no matter what anyone else thought, to the victor (and we know who they are) went the spoils. They then got to narrate the 'truth', in terms of honour, morality and worthiness, without meaningful ques-tioning under pain of outright discrimination towards anyone who defied them. Despite this, around 250 years ago, move-ments sprung up to demand more for disenfranchised people. This was quickly suppressed by a few meaningless concessions for a minority of people, appeasing the masses, but on the greater scale nothing really ever changed. Examples of this include the French Revolution, abolition of slavery, women's suffrage and the civil rights movement to name just a few.

Activists at each of these moments in history have thought, 'THIS IS IT . . . CHANGE AT LAST.' But each time nothing did, and they were always told . . . give it time. Discrimination adapted to its environment, like a Stephen King horror movie about aliens living among us who developed into us, became more perfect than us in order to exploit us; and when we adapt to challenge it, it's always one step ahead ready to thwart our efforts to break the chains at every attempt.

The roots of discrimination are fixed firmly deep in the bowels of society; while above ground it can become pliable, strong, resilient and able to morph into whatever it needs to in order to convince us it's on our side. The perfect adversary and friend at the same time. It coerces allies to do its bidding, as the Nazis did with the Vichy French, but that isn't sustainable, it will be too transparent to last for long enough and the resistance would be forever fighting against it. So, as it always has done, it shapeshifts into something else, and engages elite members of this resistance to do its bidding. In this way, the message appears to come from the disadvantaged group itself and therefore has a higher chance of the masses conceding to it. Just like Floyd Mayweather, dodging, weaving, swaying, being hit now and again but not enough to be hurt. And while it doesn't deliver a knockout blow, it will wear you down until you just go through the motions and accept the inevitability of DEFEAT.

FOUNDATIONS AND STRUCTURES OF RACISM

Even if we challenge the structures of racism, the foundation remains and foundation is much harder to dismantle than the structures. When we talk about racism and discrimination, we know there has to be a system in place that underpins and supports it. What does that system look like? The most important part is the foundation: as in any building that lasts, the foundation (which can't be seen) supports and dictates what structures can be built above ground. Now, the structures may change shape, be flexible, deceptive in their uses, but have to work in harmony and cohesion with the foundation, no matter what the illusion suggests. We have seen that for thousands of years, structures have changed but the foundation which really is the essence, stays the same. It's been about exploitation, control and discrimination of different groups. The exploited groups may have changed over thousands of years, which is when we see different structures emerge, but the foundation stays hidden away, never changing and always dictates the dynamic of the relationship between people.

The foundation has always been created by the elite of that time who produce structures to support their agendas. Then, as people who don't benefit from their agenda begin to demand more, those structures became pliable enough to superficially keep them happy, but also flexible enough to disenfranchise others who may have been elite once upon a time but are now not useful, strong or resilient enough anymore. New people will then be placed into positions of power and elevated in society. This was a perfect way to keep elitism alive. Catering to new strong groups who wanted more and were possibly capable of achieving complete overhaul of the system if their demands weren't met; this couldn't be allowed to happen, so they made sure to give out the scraps they craved.

So, the 'modern' system over the last few hundred years has looked like this: same foundation, but new and improved structures to keep noisy upstarts happy, without ever really changing anything. Because as real socialists will tell you, the only way to achieve true change is for complete and absolute overhaul of the system through revolution, and that isn't going to happen in our lifetime. Therefore, what has been happening for a long time now, is the allowance of a handful of Black people, a few women, some gay people, etc. to get involved in the structures of the system. They can never change the system, as the unseen reality hasn't changed in hundreds of years, so even the idea of dismantling structures is useless, because any new structure would have to be aligned with the foundation or else it would collapse.

Unless we expose, dig up and change the foundations, the only structures that will work are ones that, even if they give the illusion that they're different, remain in direct cohesion and alignment with the old foundations. This makes change almost impossible to accomplish as those foundations are so deep-rooted, invisible and hard to define or prove to be destructive. All we do then is continue to challenge and change structures, which fools us in the short term into thinking real change has been achieved.

The time it takes for structures to even give the impression of change is so long, that by the time we realise it hasn't actually worked, we are too old to do anything about it. Then the new, hungry, dynamic young people start out on their journey towards equality, take up the baton and start at the same place as we did, dozens of years ago.

There is a football analogy to the reality of the foundation/structure system. Take Manchester City Football Club under current manager Pep Guardiola: they have created a new system that is supported firstly by the foundation, then the structure. The foundation is rigid. We win. How do we win though? By scoring goals, by defending better than the opposition. Both valid points, but first our principles are put in place. WE DONT GIVE THE BALL AWAY! Because, before we figure out how to score more goals or defend better, if we never give the ball away in the first place then we have a better chance of doing both.

Many teams, particularly in the old days, either do crossing and shooting, or defending crossing and shooting drills because scoring goals, and not conceding goals, wins matches. But those elements in a 90-minute game constitute not even 10 per cent of the time. What do you do for the other 90 per cent of the time? Not giving the ball away gives you a better opportunity to get the ball into the right areas to enable you to score more goals. It also gives the opposition less time with the ball in their attacking areas which would enable them to score against you. So, the 'we want to score' and 'we want to stop them scoring' plan, starts for Man City with WE DONT GIVE THE BALL AWAY. That's the foundation of the team. The structure may change – personnel, shape, formation – but the foundation stays the same and they choose their players based on the foundation, which means choosing players who are comfortable in possession.

Other teams, like Atletico Madrid have a different foundation. They don't focus on keeping possession, their foundation is strength and organisation out of possession. Again, their structure in terms of personnel, shape and formation changes, but the foundation stays the same. Liverpool uses a combination of both. So, while the structures of all three teams named above may change, their foundations stay the same and that's why they are so successful. You can go back to look at the legacies of Bill Shankly, Brian Clough, Sir Alex Ferguson, Arsène Wenger or any lasting successful sporting dynasty, and you will see the harmony, relationship and cohesion between foundations and structures. And in cases of failure, it isn't just about dismantling structures, but also ripping up the foundations.

MANIPULATION OF THE WHITE, WORKING-CLASS COMMUNITIES

The white establishment cleverly tries to turn white working-class communities against Black people by saying, 'Look at them protesting but what about you?', to make them think, 'Yes, what about us?!' and then push back against the idea of Black people being discriminated against. However, the Black community aren't the ones determining the financial hardship that the white working-class endure; that's the role of the establishment and this is who they should really be angry at. Those white working-class people should say to the establishment, 'Yes, Black people are being discriminated against, and so are we, by YOU!'

The establishment has two Black allies: the first is, unwittingly, the Black extremist activist who wants to tear down statues and 'cancel' white historical heroes, who sees racism everywhere, who attacks ALL white people, even the ones who are nearly as exploited and disenfranchised as themselves. Doing this can alienate the rest of the Black community in the eyes of the white working-class, who will turn against them for being 'too radical' and demanding. In acting this way, they are given enough rope to hang themselves with (in terms of the fight for equality). The second ally is one who is entrenched in the system, professes to want change but is careful in who they criticise. They have a platform given to them by the establishment to point out and make scapegoats of people of no consequence (mainly the white working-class, Eastern Europeans, and other marginalised groups) to try to prove to other, less well-off Black people that they have their best interests at heart. In fact, the reality is that they have their own interests at heart, of course. Then, there are the people in the middle of those two aforementioned groups, a group which I include myself in, who the establishment silences as we take an objective view on race relations and understand the need for class and race to be addressed together sometimes. Some people say doing this can water down the efforts on both sides, but in fact I think it strengthens the efforts and if more disenfranchised groups were to join together in their fight, we may actually see real change.

The elite have always been aware of their sense of superiority, racially or otherwise, over the masses and have been able to hide it sufficiently so as not to be recognised to be acting this way. It is different though for white working-class people, as their perception of themselves in relation to other races has been relatively recent (the last 150 years or so). The reality of their similarity to these so-called other races is lost on them because, while their intelligence, morality or any other characteristic may be comparable to other disenfranchised groups, they have been conditioned to believe that people who look like them (elite white people) ARE truly superior. So, they are wrestling with perception over reality. This isn't helped by the fact that they are nearly equally as likely to fail as people in other disenfranchised groups because of inequalities they face due to class. This fact has actually helped the elite to push the idea of 'foreigners' being the main reason for the underprivileges that the white working-class face. On one hand, they use the working-class to maintain the status quo by subliminally encouraging hatred towards these 'foreigners' and then they punish them for carrying out racist acts. This infuriates white working-class people and further strengthens their negative stance towards the 'foreigner', and so the vicious cycle continues. Furthermore, if they are able to get ELITE members of the Black community to be the ones who make these decisions concerning who is guilty and who is not when it comes to racism, that makes the hatred towards other races even greater, as the white elite aren't being seen as the ones coming down hard on the white working-classes . . . decisions without blame!

While the British Empire sowed the seeds of racism in Britain, it didn't manifest itself until the children of the colonies started to come to Britain and impact on the local people. The exploitation of the white working-class by the elite was made all the easier by explaining away their discontent and problems with the new inhabitants. Aligned with what was taught by philosophers and scientists for the previous 200 years about the 'unworthiness' of other races, as well as propaganda in the press about colonial greatness and altruism, it became a relatively simple process to galvanise local mistrust and hatred towards other races.

GENDER INEQUALITY AND VIOLENCE AGAINST WOMEN

In the week when the body of thirty-three-year-old Sarah Everard was discovered, who was murdered by a policeman, we saw a strong response from society of people horrified by the events that had taken place. It reminded us of all the violence and harassment that women go through on a daily basis throughout their lives. The media feasted on this story, and everyone said, 'enough is enough', 'we must all do more', 'now is the time'.

During a vigil carried out at London's Clapham Common, which the police had tried to disperse, the image of a woman pinned to the ground and handcuffed by a police officer quickly became viral online and in all media outlets. The narrative following this incident was along the lines of, 'This feels different!' Sound familiar? Just like the George Floyd incident felt different; but time passes and the passion, anger and motivation of society wanes until the only reminder is a token symbol such as footballers taking a knee on the pitch.

After the vigil there were calls for Cressida Dick, commissioner of the Metropolitan Police, to resign due to what was described as 'heavy-handed policing' of the event. People stated that because she's a woman she should empathise with other women and do more to support their plight, which the vigil was attempting to highlight. Another woman in leadership who receives criticism along these lines is Kamala Harris, Vice President of the United States and previous attorney general and US senator. She comes under fire because she is Black and was part of a system that disproportionally imprisons Black people. In any situation like this, what we have to understand is that the person, be it Cressida Dick or Kamala Harris, is part of a system that favours MEN and WHITE people, so it's impossible for them as individuals to do anything to change that. This was even the same for Barack Obama, who was at one point arguably the most powerful man in the world.

Many people feel passionate about the need for the criminal justice system to change regarding women and people of colour. However, as I've said all along, changing or implementing laws alone won't work. How long has it been illegal to rape, abuse and harass women, or to racially discriminate against people? But this still continues. Not only are the conviction rates low, but so are reporting rates. And why is this? Because the burden of proof falls on the victim . . . the woman, the Black person, the Muslim person. We live in a society that presumes innocent until proven guilty, and while the burden of proof is on the victim, the law also protects the guilty if there is not enough solid evidence to convict. Because the law (which is part of our society) is designed to favour white people and men, it's no surprise that it becomes hard under these laws to prove that those groups are guilty in the majority of cases.

So just like in racism towards footballers, if you commit overt acts such as throwing a banana on the field or shouting racist abuse to a player, or the murder of Stephen Lawrence or George Floyd, those acts can be dealt with by punishment and imprisonment. But these aren't the systemic discriminations that affect women or Black people as a whole on a daily basis. Just like so many white people will say, 'Well, I don't shout racist abuse or throw bananas on the field so I'm not racially biased', some men say, in the same vein, 'Well, I would never rape or murder a woman, or shout out sexual innuendos at them, therefore I'm not sexist.' It is these people who are the obstacles to equality for disenfranchised people. Those who don't understand that by just avoiding overt actions of discrimination this does not equate to creating a better society with equal opportunities. Instead of changing laws, we have to change our perception of firstly, what is racism, what is sexism, etc? And secondly, we must address, challenge and change why we feel the way we do towards people who are different to us, be they people of a different, race, sexuality, gender or religious group.

In the example of gender inequality, the solution has to come from the people in power, the majority, those who actually have the ability to affect change – and that group is MEN. Women forcing men to change without getting them to fully understand the reasons why they need to, will always be difficult. How many times do we hear the phrase, 'Not all men . . .', just like, 'Not all white people . . .'? This defensive response is useless, unhelpful and shows a lack of understanding that we need to change.

I can completely understand and empathise with what women are going through. If you analyse my previous comments, you can see that both Black people and women go through similar experiences, although there is less overt denial regarding the plight of women. In society today, everyone has to be seen to believe and sympathise with the experiences of women – however, that feeling is not the same regarding the experiences of Black people. Is it surprising then, that with what appears to be such widespread support and belief of women, there are so few reports, never mind convictions, of sexual assault? It is because no matter what we say, the fact is that the law is designed to protect men.

So, if we need to look at society as a whole before we condemn the institutions that appear to foster racial, gender, sexual and other forms of discrimination, perhaps the lessons of history can serve as a wake-up call and provide some insight into how our thoughts and values have been conditioned.

PART TWO

'To be free is not merely to cast off one's chains,

but to live in a way that respects and

enhances the freedom of others.'

Nelson Mandela

4

WHAT EMPIRE AND COLONIALISM HAVE TAUGHT US

How does anyone convince the majority of people that they are doing the right thing? Firstly, once the perception of 'what is right' is completely intertwined with 'as long as it is us who's doing it', you can get away legally, morally or ethically with anything. And this has been the case from time immemorial. Consider the example of how British 'free trade' worked in the mid-nineteenth century.

The Opium Wars in China (which showed Britain's 'superiority' in the face of provocation) preceded the securing of Hong Kong as an overseas territory. Britain used to trade silver with China, in exchange for superior Eastern goods. When silver became less accessible to Britain, they needed something which would be seen as equally valuable, so they started to trade a commodity harvested in India (another of their overseas territories), opium. This proved lucrative, but the Chinese complained that their people were becoming addicted and were dying in their thousands. How dare the Chinese complain about this – this is free trade! The trading wasn't being done by the British government, but by the East India Company, albeit with royal patronage. The Chinese burnt a couple of the British ships carrying opium and threw the opium overboard in protest. The white traders from the East India Company then wanted compensation from the British government because they had guaranteed freedom of trade with China. That proved to be too expensive, so the easier solution would be to force the Chinese people to accept the trading of opium. So, the British blockaded the harbour, started a war, won the war and free trade of opium started again.

Following this the British were hailed as heroes for free trade, and stories of greatness, honour and valour were told. I'm sure many men were knighted, with honours and favours bestowed upon our great heroes for defeating the 'evil' Chinese.

Opium trading was illegal in Britain, as was slavery; however, it was legal in the colonies. Isn't it interesting that when someone knows something is wrong, they ban it among themselves, but because it's lucrative, allow it among people they control and therefore ultimately profit from the activity? How can you convince the majority that you are right in the actions you undertake solely on the basis of 'if we do it, it's alright'?

Here is a modern-day fictional extrapolation of the Opium Wars. Pablo Escobar, head of the Colombian Medellín cartel, wants to trade cocaine with the US by sailing up the Hudson river to Manhattan. President Donald Trump is against this because, 'our blond-haired blue-eyed people are dying in their thousands from it'. Pablo Escobar says he doesn't care because there is a market for it and 'we have a trade agreement'. Donald says, 'That's just for Colombian coffee.' Pablo replies, 'Trade is trade.' Donald states, 'Isn't it illegal in your own country?'. Pablo responds, 'It's a bad signal, no network coverage, I can't hear you . . .' Pablo goes to the president of Colombia and tells him that the Americans are throwing his drugs into the Hudson. The Colombian president sends his war ships to Manhattan and forces the US to trade cocaine with Pablo. Sounds outrageous, right?

If you think about all the stories of 'honourable conquest' by Western powers over the last 400 years, using the story above as a reference point, what do you think is the likelihood that the reaction to Colombia's actions would be similar to the praises given following Britain's actions in the Opium Wars? Unlikely.

The same thing happened in America towards immigrants, when racially motivated attacks occurred openly because the majority of people and the rhetoric from the administration said 'they' are the problem. People felt empowered to openly, and without fear of prosecution, attack 'those' people who they were told were the source of their discontent.

Capitalism and free trade helped create European 'Empires' some 500 years ago, giving nations like Britain strategic, financial and logistic power over the rest of the world. This fed a sense of superiority over others, especially non-white populations. But 100 years earlier, the Chinese started that idea under their maritime leader Zheng He who travelled with hundreds of huge ships throughout Southeast Asia and East Africa to establish trade relations with local governments. Being more advanced and more powerful than the people they were trading with, the Chinese merchants subsequently became very rich. As time moved on, however, the Chinese government back home began to fear that the merchants would not only get disproportionately richer than the rest of society, but also become too powerful politically and be able to exert too much pressure on the government to their own benefit, which would be detrimental to the majority of ordinary people. So they burned the overseas ships and storehouses, banned foreign trade and instead concentrated on land trade with their immediate neighbours. The Europeans, in contrast, continued their foreign trading exploits down the centuries and we see the way the world is now, not only for the conquered people but also for the majority of working-class people within those European countries regarding the inequity of wealth.

We in the West have to wake up and understand that although we feel that the rest of the world still looks upon us as the beacon of right-mindedness, we are only fooling ourselves. The rest of the world didn't have a choice but to be subservient, and until the day comes again where 'might is right' (post-Trump the Americans in particular might be reappraising this approach) they can no longer be bullied into doing what we say or be tricked into believing that we are 'doing them a favour' by offering a few crumbs. It's our arrogance, stemming from our perception of ourselves in relation to others that we subconsciously feel that as long as it's us saying or doing it, it will be accepted. That feeling may also be shared among many people in the developing world; however there is an independent elite who feel just as empowered, educated and worthy as their Western counterparts.

So, take stable Middle Eastern countries, for example. Once upon a time the West may have been able to completely exploit them by making out that they were doing them a favour, while giving them scraps from the table. Now, while the West still exerts some influence over them, the spoils are shared in a much different way.

Here in the UK, we talk a lot about the effect slavery has had on racism, and as far as scientific racism and racial bias by the elite goes, that was the main reason that it was adopted and why it spread so easily. We don't address what in my opinion has created racial bias within the majority of the people, that is much more impactful today, and that is colonialism.

THE SLAVE TRADE

Slavery was started, and continued, by individuals and corporations who benefited from that institution. While governments reaped the fruits through taxes and other 'gifts' granted, and cities grew in wealth through adopting other industries off the back of the profits from the goods the slaves produced, the British government itself, while supporting and facilitating the slave trade, didn't engage in the trade itself – it was private enterprise. So, after the scientists and philosophers created a myth about the inferiority of the races, which satisfied the so-called right-minded aristocracy and elite that they were not doing anything wrong morally or ethically, it had free reign to exploit and mistreat Black people without any feeling of guilt.

This continued from the sixteenth century all the way up to the end of slavery, when it was abolished in Britain by the Slavery Abolition Act of 1833. There was no need for the average person in the UK, or even the absentee slave owners (those in the UK who owned slaves, but never even set foot in the Caribbean . . . and there were plenty) to even contemplate whether racial bias played a part in their lives. They were reaping the rewards of slavery by starting up other business with the profits, doing good work in their communities by helping poor white working-class people and opening schools and shops. All while never having to think about the horrors of slavery, or whether the Black slaves were inferior human beings or not.

How could that be? Today, we are full witness to the horrors of slavery: the tracking, killing and capturing of whole villages in West Africa, and beyond; the brutality of bodies chained together, people squashed in the hold of the slave ships like sardines, sometimes with only two feet of space between them for months on end at sea; the parade of naked, bruised, pus-infected bodies being presented in a square for sale. Back then, the average person didn't see these atrocious conditions, or I would like to think they would have condemned this type of treatment of other human beings. They would not have treated animals in that way never mind other humans, even Black ones.

Why didn't they know? The transatlantic slave trade started with an empty slave ship, containing only guns, alcohol or other worthless trinkets, leaving England reaching the west coast of Africa and trading these items for captured slaves. They sailed across the Atlantic with those unfortunate mistreated souls, selling them in the New World (or to absentee slave holders in the UK). The ships would then take the spoils of the slaves' work (cotton, sugar, tobacco and other commodities) and triumphantly return to the UK to sell these wonderful products that magically appeared at our ports like manna from heaven, with the average person not realising how they came about. This radically changed Britain and made life more comfortable for everyone, as well as producing more jobs and opportunities for many more people. Race, never mind racism, never entered the minds of the vast majority of British people at this time.

Towards the end of the slave trade when questions started to be asked, scientific and philosophical claptrap was spued out to justify these actions, until the religious question of man's inhumanity to each other won the day. The question of equality was never debated or discussed, just the moral question as to whether slavery was right, even for 'unequal' people. In other words, not much different to what we are mistakenly trying to do today.

THE EMPIRE STRIKES BACK

So, slavery was abolished and the world should have been a better place for Black people in the colonies, Africa and even in Britain. At that point we accepted the fact that Black people deserved better, but importantly not that they were equal, just that they didn't deserve to be enslaved and mistreated. With the lucrative slave trade now abolished and the government needing to pay reparations to slave owners (which have only recently been paid off), they saw an opportunity to make even more money by expanding the Empire further. The government had already seen the financial benefits of the Empire that India brought, as originally this was private enterprise through the East India Company, then taken over by Britain itself. So, they decided, along with other European countries, to carve up Africa, exploiting its rich natural resources at a much larger and more profitable scale than the transatlantic slave trade did.

How were they going to do that after it was decided that the exploitation of Black people was morally and ethically wrong? Before Victorian times, there wasn't necessarily a feeling of pride among the working-class society of Britain for 'just being British'. It was the aristocracy, the elite and the growing middle class who benefited from what slavery and the limited Empire gave. The working-class were given scraps which made them content, but the overseas endeavours never captured their imagination. To embark on a much larger Empire-building enterprise, you needed many more working-class people to sign up to serve, so that's when the whole nation had to be convinced to support colonialism. Queen Victoria became Empress of India, and the propaganda machine went into overdrive. This not only told people to support activities by the government abroad, but also convinced them of the altruistic, benevolent and moral obligation to 'help those poor, foreign savages' to improve their lot. To achieve this, they had to create the feeling of superiority among even the poor, white working-class, which they did in the late nineteenth century through excessive propaganda in the form of postcards, cigarette cards, films, theatre productions showing glorious battles and benevolent missions. Here inferior Black, Indian and Chinese people were ridiculed and mistreated while the white man taught and civilised them, alongside the general 'glory of the British Empire' narrative. All of this was consumed by the average white working-class person who could now identify with the superiority of 'being British'. So how could this average British person not feel superior? That was when the idea of racial superiority among most, if not all, British people took root subliminally. This feeling continued while most colonies gained independence from Britain and still strongly remains today.

Now that Black, Asian, Muslim, and other previously colonised people live among white British people, why are things not getting better regarding race relations? Exploitation has always been more of a class rather than race issue, and racism within communities was never an issue until the end of Empire, when people from the former colonies came to live among the working class. This feeling of superiority towards them was already there from the previous fifty years, as life got worse for the working class and they found themselves no better off economically than the people they felt superior to. There had to be a reason why that was, surely? This isn't what they had supported the glorious Empire for, to be the same as these inferior people!

Once the idea of racial superiority was well-established in the British psyche, even before independence came to the colonies, hundreds of British citizens then moved to the colonies to work for British companies and government entities. They worked among the local populations, sometimes doing the exact same jobs, administratively, technically and manually, but received more pay.

RACIAL SUPERIORITY TAKES HOLD

The different ideas of what human beings feel they 'need' or 'deserve' for doing the same job and their 'requirements' is worth mentioning. Why does a Black man in Nigeria, with a wife, mortgage and three children, not need, deserve or require the same salary as a white man who moved to Nigeria and has the same mid-level civil service job with a wife, mortgage and three kids? Our views towards this stem from not only the exploitative nature of the financial world, but also of the perception of worth and needs endowed upon different races.

Years later, when immigrants came to Britain in the '60s, they were paid a particular wage, which British people were originally happy to work for before the immigrants came. Then when the British realised that these immigrants were receiving the same as them, suddenly that wasn't enough. It wasn't necessarily the amount; it was the fact that they unconsciously felt they deserved more than the immigrant because of their superiority. This shows how the conditioning of racial superiority took hold without many even being aware of it.

Racial inequality, depending on how you describe race, is one of the biggest issues in the world today. The current status quo has been the norm for hundreds of years; it was challenged by former colonies of European nations after the shackles of colonialism were thrown off, but this didn't affect the balance of power or the pro-European narrative within these countries themselves. To a certain extent the Western nations controlled, and still do today, not only the narrative but the political and economic dynamic of the former colonies. The problem for the powerbrokers is the children of the former colonies, born and brought up in Europe and the US and, to all intents and purposes, 'European' or 'American', but who are treated like the countrymen of the former colonies. These new populations won't put up with it anymore, as they know their worth because they are constantly being told that they should be treated as equals.

This fight really is a Western issue, as it appears that the demands for equality are most apparent among Black people, women and other disenfranchised groups in the UK, US or

European countries. Regardless of the fact that the biggest problems for those groups are still in the former colonies, those affected in the mother countries seem to forget this and want equality for themselves and the elite few rather than the silent voiceless majority.

We should focus on the legacy of colonialism and slavery rather than colonialism and slavery itself. Because the legacy is actually much more impactful on the present world regarding racism and exploitation rather than the act itself. The act itself has nothing to do with today's society and therefore people nowadays can feel comfortable in knowing they weren't around back then and can't be to blame for the past. In this way, the reality of racial inequality can feel like a distant memory, despite the fact that its legacy is the sole reason for those inequalities.

People generally believe in togetherness, peace, community and harmony: that's how we have survived as the human race for so long. We believe in working together for the good of the group. But greed was and still is the main reason for wanting more than the next person. It's not in our nature to be greedy, it feels uncomfortable, so we don't want to see the negative effects our greed has on our neighbour. In that case, the best way to make ourselves feel okay about our greed, is if we ignore, or simply don't look for those negative impacts we have on the people we exploit. To do this, rather than exploiting our neighbours in Scotland, Wales and Ireland, where due to proximity we would see and feel the tangible guilt of doing so, instead it's easier for us to exploit, inflict pain and suffering on groups who the vast majority of us will never physically see. That is how we were able to silently colonise the world while all the 'right-minded' people back in England could ignore the negative effects of our actions in the colonies because not only could they not see these consequences, but they were sold on the 'glory' of it and reaped the benefits back at home. That was the clear advantage of exploiting people far away geographically, then creating a philosophy of those people being far away from us racially, so as to once again lessen our guilt of exploiting our common man. Britain, as an isolated island, was ideally placed for the average person's eyes to be closed to the horrors that were forced upon people from distant lands. These people were perceived as distant races and not people we could empathise with, or else they would have been horrified.

There is no better way to change people's minds than to actually show them the horror or glory of something. By telling stories alone, we feel the bias of the victors, whereas our eyes cannot deceive us. So, for example, while some of mainstream

America may have supported the IRA through hearing biased stories, despite them being viewed as a terrorist group by some, it took the horrors of terrorism actually reaching their own shores, in the form of the 9/11 terror attack, for them to change their perceptions.

If the Western world was to physically see and feel the horrors of slavery, child labour in India, insurgency in Iraq, religious wars in the Middle East, poverty in the majority of sub-Saharan African countries – many of these issues actually caused by Western countries themselves – their conscience and right-mindedness would compel them to do something about it and not accept it. America, again with its geographic isolation, is similar and has learnt from its cousins about exploiting people as far away from home as possible. In doing so, it's easier to create the illusion of being the benefactors to others and helping them out of their backwardness.

Imagine if, during the transatlantic slave trade, rather than millions of slaves being transported from Africa straight to the US and the Caribbean, they were instead brought first back to Britain? For British people to see these Black African people after months at sea, stuffed together like sardines, beaten in chains, kept in warehouses waiting to be sold in public squares, marched naked in shackles through the streets of London to the docks only then to be transported to the US and the Caribbean. Then after seeing all of this, the British people would be told not to worry as the slaves would be sold for sugar, tobacco, cotton and other beautiful goods that would be brought back to British shores in six months. Do you think transatlantic slavery would have lasted for 300 years? No way. People would not have accepted it after seeing such horrific scenes with their own eyes. But, as with many issues to do with race and discrimination, it's out of sight, out of mind.

5

'I DON'T SEE *YOU* AS BLACK'

HOW WE SEE OURSELVES

I have talked a lot about people using the phrase, 'I don't see *you* as Black', and the problem with this. Just like the question, 'Can Black players become good managers?'. It's bullshit. I always felt that having that uncomfortable discussion with my white friends would embarrass them. When you say, 'I don't see *you* as Black', you think you're using it as a compliment. If I were to ask a friend truly what they saw me as, they would likely want to respond with (and this has actually been said to me before without any thought of how it sounds), 'I see you as normal.'

I would then say, 'Really, is Black not normal then?'

Uncomfortable silence to follow. I would then become a bit provocative. 'If you don't see me as being Black, then what is your perception of Black that I am not?'

I would go on, 'Is it because I don't wear my jeans round my arse and have a spliff out my mouth and am reasonably intelligent?'

Then to ease the discomfort and diffuse the situation, I would laugh and say, 'I'm only joking', to let him off the hook.

The idea for this book really came about because I've been travelling around the world for the last seven or eight years with work. To give you an idea of the extent of my travels I've had around 250 flights in less than three years – not to Spain and France, but to African countries mainly, China, Australia, Indonesia, the Middle East and Southeast Asia. Long trips to really faraway places. As a consequence of these very long flights, I read a lot to pass the time. Never fiction, but books on sociology, philosophy, anthropology or history and I have become worryingly interested in the way the world works. Noam Chomsky has had a huge impact on the way I think. With so much flying, I've seen many different groups of people, and through people-watching and observing their different characteristics and personality traits, to my surprise I had a eureka moment: WE'RE ALL THE SAME!

We can learn a lot from people in airports and on aeroplanes, from Johannesburg to Accra, Beijing to Kuala Lumpur, Sydney to Dubai, Jakarta to Dar es Salaam. People like to travel, kids make noise and are sometimes a nuisance on planes; people like to shop; they get pissed off; they're kind; they're mean; they get tired, angry, happy, sad. I could go on. Some have turbans, some hijabs, pink hair, traditional African dress, three-piece suits, leather trousers. Different characters, different upbringings, different cultures, different beliefs, the list is endless. But let there be a delay on a flight and we're all the same. Let there be bad turbulence and we're all the same. Let there be a drunk passenger or a crying baby, we all have the same reactions (myself excluded – I have seven kids so can empathise with child and parent).

Coming into contact with so many different groups of people and seeing the inherent similarities between us has had a profound effect on the way I view people now. So, ultimately, to win the fight against unconscious racism, which is the most prevalent type, what has to change is not our perception of any individual 'Black' person, but our perception of what 'Black' means to us.

UNCONSCIOUS BIAS

I am a product of my British upbringing so identify with people like me – not just Black, but English in terms of language, culture, humour, dress, attitude, etc. All it takes for anyone to identify with someone else is a commonality or a feeling of fraternity. If you can get that feeling, you will accept anyone as being 'just like you', or at least view them less suspiciously.

This is where football comes in. Contrary to popular belief, Asians love football, Arabs love football, everyone loves football. And on the odd occasion I get recognised by someone in, for example, traditional Sikh dress with a turban who then approaches me to talk about how much he loves Liverpool and remembers the '89 Cup Final, or asks why I didn't take the ball into the corner flag against Arsenal in the last minute to win the league, I immediately identify and feel a bond with that person, even just for a minute. This happens with Chinese people, Africans, Orthodox Jews, the list goes on.

The point I'm making is that my perception of those particular groups of people can change after I have a very short conversation with them about football. After seeing them in the same environment as me and seeing the way they react to similar situations in exactly the same way I do, it has made me question whether there are any real differences between us, what causes us to feel different from each other.

I believe that the main cause of these perceived differences is, once again, what we have been told not only about each other, but also about ourselves. The best way I can try to convince you that there is a common essence to humanity with an inherent identity among us all, is to tell a story I like to call, 'Life is like a broken elevator.'

Picture this: Her Majesty The Queen and her aides, Donald Trump and the Secret Service, a painter, a lawyer, a taxi driver, a homeless man, a middle-class Black man, a working-class Black man, a Muslim, a Jewish person, a homosexual man and a woman get in an elevator. The Queen and her aides keep well away from everyone else, as does Donald Trump and the Secret Service. The painter and taxi driver probably talk to each other and the lawyer hovers between the groups. The homeless man stands alone in the corner and everyone else mills around minding their own business.

The elevator gets stuck, and for the first five minutes nothing changes with respect to where everyone is positioned, then as time goes on, it gets hot and sticky, so the Queen's aides and Secret Service loosen their ties and start to talk to each other. The painter and taxi driver join in; they talk about their kids, wives, football. Donald Trump then talks about Ivanka, his kids and grabbing p***y (sorry, not really). The Queen talks about Charles, her grandkids, etc. The two Black guys start up a conversation; the woman and the homosexual man move towards each other; the Muslim stands alone; the Jewish person goes over to Donald Trump.

The middle-class Black guy talking to the working-class Black guy finds out that, while he likes Black Sabbath, the working-class Black guy likes classical music; he likes rugby, and the other likes chess. He realises they have nothing in common apart from the colour of their skin, so he goes looking for someone else to talk with. The woman asks the homosexual man if he has any lip balm she could borrow, the homosexual man says he left it at the boxing gym where he was training earlier. The Muslim gets some water out of the rucksack he was carrying and his season ticket at Anfield falls out. One of the Secret Service guys says he supports Liverpool as well and they strike up a conversation about who was the best Liverpool striker, Rush, Suárez or Torres. The taxi driver asks the painter if he saw the fight the other night, but he says no because he was at his salsa class, but the homosexual man saw it, and thought that the referee should never have stopped it. They get hotter and sweatier and all start to smell like the homeless man.

Another thirty minutes go by, someone farts and they all laugh; it's the Queen (she does fart you know). The Secret Service isn't protecting Donald Trump now; they're playing cards with the Muslim man and the taxi driver. The Queen's aides aren't seeing to the Queen; they're seeing who can throw a coin closet to the lift door with the working-class Black guy. The homeless man is telling Donald and the Queen that he was a hairdresser before falling on hard times and lost his salon, house and family due to alcoholism; he's sharing this information not for money or sympathy, just to pass the time. They are now all the same – hot, hungry, sweaty, smelly, with differing likes and dislikes – people stuck in a lift, some with a lot in common, but not necessarily with the ones they thought.

All of a sudden, the lift starts moving again. The Queen's aides do up their ties and attend to the Queen; she straightens herself up; the Secret Service surrounds Donald who puts his toupee back on; the painter and taxi driver exchange numbers; the two Black guys fist bump; the woman and homosexual man straighten themselves up; the homeless man wanders over to the corner. They all revert to who they think they should be or who the world tells them they are. So, when the lift door opens and the world's media sees them, all is as expected to be.

They emerge and the Queen goes to her Rolls Royce; Donald's helicopter whisks him off; the lawyer jumps into a Black cab and the painter jumps into the taxi driver's cab to go off for a pint. The homeless man skulks away to find the bin where he left his McDonald's.

While they all go back to their very different environments, and despite the perception the world has of them, the perception 'they' will forever have of 'each other' will be that for a brief period in time, they absolutely identified with each other, and were all exactly the same: HOT, SMELLY, SWEATY PEOPLE STUCK IN A LIFT.

The saying that you should never meet your heroes because you'll be disappointed can be true; but there are two different perspectives to this saying. First perspective: John Barnes is your hero; you meet him and he is normal, just like you, sitting in economy on a plane, in an old T-shirt, baggy tracksuit and flip flops. And after talking to him, he goes on way too much about his kids and bores you to death. If you wanted that, you'd talk to your boring mates; you want to hear about glamourous stuff, his superstar mates and the celebrity life he leads to let you know he's better than you. What a let-down.

Second perspective: John Barnes is your hero; you meet him and he is arrogant, flashy, sitting in first class (unfortunately this doesn't happen, not these days, but I can dream and it's my story), snubs you at first but then proceeds to tell you about his goals, cars, houses, meeting up with Jay Z and Beyoncé then calls his security because more fans are flocking around him. What a superstar! You'd be surprised at the number of people who would be more impressed with the second John Barnes, if he existed.

You may remember seeing footage that went viral of a white man doing a serious Skype interview with BBC News in his study in South Korea, when a toddler wanders into the background, quickly followed by an Asian woman who frantically ushers the child out. It was hilarious. Then uproar started when some people concluded she was the nanny, and presumably petrified that her 'boss' would be angry that the child had interrupted his work. But she turned out to be his wife. My initial thought also was, 'She's the nanny', and I'm sure the majority of people also thought this. So why are we pretending that we don't all make uninformed generalisations based on race, and only accuse others of being racist? This is what we have become because of stereotypical attitudes that the majority of us have. We have all been conditioned to think a certain way because of what we have learned, seen and experienced.

While you may feel the context of this book is white/Black based, it isn't, it's about stereotypical assumptions of different groups of people, and the impact it has on all of us.

Take Southeast Asia for example. I've been going there for thirty years and one of the observations that stands out a mile is young, beautiful, local girls being on the arm of white, average-looking, middle-aged men. You may also remember old Vietnam War films of the pretty girls in the company of GIs from America. These pairings may have been easier to understand years ago, as during and immediately after colonial times, women all over (not just in Southeast Asia) were drawn to powerful, successful men regardless of age or attraction; and the majority of white men in developing countries were the wealthy successful types.

Things have changed since those days: you now may see relatively poor, uneducated, 'average' white men in these developing countries, the majority of them definitely punching above their weight, as we say. This is because of the local society's perception of them as a white man as being 'superior' and therefore desirable, and also (although they wouldn't admit it), the unconscious perception they have of themselves. By that, I mean how much confidence must they have to approach beautiful, successful Asian women, while being average-looking white guys who couldn't find work in the UK, for example, so emigrated to Singapore to sleep on their brothers' couch, yet still feel that these women will go out with them? I'm using this as a generalised example of course, not applicable in all cases. What do they think they have to offer, or why do they feel these women will be attracted to them? They very well might be successful, and in that case their confidence won't be dented by rejection. Why is that? That's because they know full well (albeit unconsciously most of the time) that there are no restrictions on what the world has to offer them as white men, and if they persevere, they can eventually be successful, believing it's based on their own personal merit rather than any advantage they may have over others due to the colour of their skin.

It's also interesting to look at the relationship and interaction between white mid-level executives and the local population in these countries. In Singapore, the local English language is sometimes called 'Singlish' (a mixture of English and Singapore

English) and when English men speak to taxi drivers, food vendors, menial workers, they converse with them in this condescending and mocking tone. That local person accepts it and says nothing about it even if he feels it's insulting.

However, when these English men speak to locals who they consider to be more important, businesspeople, for example, they speak properly. You may think it's meaningless, and done unconsciously, but it isn't. Otherwise, they would speak Singlish all the time to every local, but they know deep down it is condescending and rude and they know who they can and can't do it to.

No matter who you are or where you're from, Singapore, Africa, the Middle East, if you get into a taxi in London and mock the driver, by putting on what you consider to be your best cockney accent, what do you think the outcome would be? Not only would you be out on your ear, but that taxi driver would have the backing and support of everyone, because 'Who do you think you are?' and 'How dare you mock him just because he's a taxi driver?'

When we judge ourselves or people like us in relation to other people, that judgement isn't just based on us as individuals; it's based on our expectations of ourselves yes, but also of the wider group and the perception we have of them. Take for example a marine who was tried and sentenced for 'murdering' a Taliban fighter (later reduced to manslaughter on the grounds of diminished responsibility). I don't know the exact laws with regard to murdering someone in war; however, apparently it was classified as such because the Taliban fighter was already captured and not a threat at that time. Without knowing too much about the specifics, let's talk about it from a human perspective. If the roles were reversed and it was a Taliban fighter who murdered a captured British marine, we would be horrified and disgusted, but we wouldn't be surprised. We also wouldn't judge him in the same way we would judge our own, because 'that's what they are like'. Whereas we feel we are better than that and would never do such a thing. So, we judge two human beings who commit the same act in different ways based on our differing perceptions of the morality, right-mindedness and honour of the group they belong to. American comedian/commentator Bill Maher refers to this phenomenon as the 'soft bigotry of low expectations'.

I have watched the first interview with this marine after he was freed from jail and the interviewer asks him why he shot the injured, unarmed Taliban fighter. He struggles to give an answer, repeatedly saying he doesn't know why, yet he continuously is asked how could he have done it. You can see he's in turmoil over his actions. The true reason he's in turmoil is because he has been told that he should be better than that, but the reality is he isn't. I know the reason he did it: because he's HUMAN.

It's the same in football, when foreign players 'cheat' by diving or feigning injury – we say, 'they're all like that', but we don't accept it from our British players, because we are 'better than that'. There are so many examples like this, whereby we make decisions on someone's worth based on perceptions of the group to which they belong (religious, racial, whatever) rather than the actual individual's qualities.

It stems from our historical account of society, which obviously has been exaggerated positively towards ourselves, and nega-tively towards others. Our perception of ourselves and others started hundreds of years ago, not through our own personal experiences or interaction with each other, but through songs, stories and books written by a few people about encounters with 'inferior' races, and how they overcame them due to their 'superiority'. That meant nothing to the vast majority of people in England and the rest of Europe, whose lives were nothing like the people who actually told those tales – given that they were poor, disenfranchised, living in virtual serfdom and also considered inferior by the aristocracy and intelligentsia. As time went on and the Enlightenment brought about a change in man's vision of himself and his worth as an individual, these tales of greatness were vicariously adopted by the average white man who was swept along with this notion of superiority, although he himself may not have achieved or accomplished anything of note, morally, intellectually or otherwise.

The feeling of superiority is based on our unconscious perception of ourselves in relation to others, and I suppose that is why I didn't feel that racism impacted on me during my football career; because of the unconscious perception I had of myself in relation to those 'racist' football fans who hurled abuse and threw bananas at me.

I've told you about my upbringing in Jamaica, which fully empowered me as a middle-class boy from a distinguished, educated family. I have, and had, a perception of who I am, so when an uneducated, stupid racist abuses me, how can I be insulted by someone like that, who I feel superior to? As a foot-baller that was a fairly easy reaction for me to have because, up to that point, life hadn't shown me anything to make me feel inferior because of my colour, and while I, even back then, understood the reality of the Black/white dynamic, personally I hadn't been affected by it.

After my formative years, I was always to society 'John Barnes the footballer' so even after football when I, like many other Black ex-players, found it hard to stay in the game, I'm still 'John Barnes the footballer'. As such, certain privileges have been afforded to me based on that, with me being 'elevated out of Blackness'.

I completely empathise with Black players/people who feel differently when faced with racist abuse, and with regard to Black players who react in a different way, it's interesting to understand why they feel the way they do. Earning hundreds of thousands of pounds per week, living in mansions, driving Aston Martins, being accepted in upper-crust social circles, while their abusers may be poor, stupid, immoral louts. Why shouldn't they feel superior to those football fans?

This feeling of superiority may well be a natural emotion to have, but it never was, nor should it be, based on race. If it has to be based on anything, shouldn't it be based on personal individual achievement? While the anthropologists and philosophers of hundreds of years ago, wrongly ascribed to humans intellectual and moral characteristics based on race (which continue today), negative characteristics like laziness, deceitfulness, savagery, etc. apply to all of humanity regardless of race depending on the experiences, environment and conditions in which one finds oneself.

BEING BLACK IN AMERICA

Black Americans today are called 'African Americans' and American Indians are now called 'Native Americans'. Not being American, I don't know if this change was made at the behest of the affected races. Do Black Americans feel more empowered by being called, or insisting on being called African Americans? I can't answer that. However, it seems taking race aside, the ideal of that country is to be an 'American', and Black/African Americans are generally very patriotic when competing in sport against other countries for example, and also in their relationships with other Black people across the world. Their 'Americanness' gives them perhaps an unconscious feeling of superiority. So, this feeling of 'Americanness' makes all Americans feel a little more superior when comparing themselves with others, albeit, even if they're unequal among themselves. So, the mainstream (white) American society are quite happy for Black Americans to insist on being called African Americans and for those we knew as American Indians to be called Native Americans. But importantly, the white 'European Americans' just get to be called 'Americans'. Because who are the world's leaders? The Americans: not African Americans, not Native Americans, just Americans.

If, as a Black person from America, you were asked to explain who you were and where you came from, saying you were 'American' would be an adequate explanation; no need to include information on your ancestral origins, as it's obvious that you originate from Africa because of your skin colour. This is also the case with the Native Americans. So, why don't white Americans say whether they are German, English, French, Polish or Russian-American? Some Americans of Italian descent do still refer to themselves as Italian American, but not as many. But to explain who they really are, shouldn't white Americans prefix 'America' with the country their ancestors originated from? They don't, because what gives them their perceived superiority is not their ancestral origins, but their 'Americanness'. So, are they the true 'Americans'? Obviously not. 'Americanness' is not considered to be a nationality but a superior state of mind and a club for the elite who only certain groups can join.

'I'M NOT RACIST/HOMOPHOBIC/SEXIST BUT . . .'

We all discriminate and there are degrees of discrimination. We are all racially biased, sexist, homophobic to a certain degree; perhaps not all three for everyone but I'm sure 99 per cent of us subconsciously discriminate in at least one of these areas, especially when we aren't personally affected by a particular one. We as Black people have all heard the statement, 'I'm not racist but . . .', homosexuals have heard, 'I'm not homophobic but . . .' and women have heard, 'I'm not sexist but . . .'. Halfway along the spectrum, you have people who say, 'I'm not racist but . . . if I'm at the airport and I see a Muslim with a big beard and a rucksack, I might get slightly uncomfortable', or 'I'm not homophobic but . . . if I'm in the toilet in a club and an obviously gay guy comes in and speaks to me, I'm a bit uncomfortable' or 'I'm not sexist but . . . if there is a woman refereeing a Premier League football match, I question more of her decisions than I would a male referee'. At the severe end of the spectrum, there are those who will say, 'All Muslims are terrorists' or 'I like to beat up homosexuals' or 'Women have no place in football'. Then you have the enlightened with no bias who say, 'I see all people as equal' and mean it, 'I'm straight and have no negative feelings in any situation towards homosexuals' and mean it and 'Women are as capable as men as far as football refereeing is concerned', and mean it.

I believe that the vast majority of people are like me though, somewhere along that spectrum with regard to many different groups. So, are we racist, homophobic and sexist? Absolutely, to a certain degree, because of the way we have been indoctrinated by society throughout our lives. But because society tells us that it won't tolerate any form of sexism, racism or homophobia, we all deny it. Rather than owning it and saying, don't blame me, this is what society has wrongly told me, and continues to tell and show me, about those groups and a host of others. So, the equality I'm fighting for is the social, moral, and intellectual form . . . which isn't based on race, religion, sex or sexual orientation.

BLACK ON WHITE RACISM

While having discussions with white friends about racism, the subject of racism towards white people often comes up. Yes, there are different kinds of racism, but are some worse than others? We've already established that there are degrees of racism, but there are also huge differences between white and

Black racism. White on Black racism is based on a perception of moral, social and intellectual superiority over that particular group. On the other hand, Black on white racism isn't based on any such feeling. It's based on what they feel, rightly or wrongly, that white people have done to them, and people like them.

It's interesting being a Black 'celebrity'. Since I've retired from playing football and now travel the world, sometimes people recognise me in the most far-flung places. They will say inquisitively, 'Did you used to be John Barnes?' I love that saying as it sums up 'celebrity-dom' perfectly. I always reply, 'That's showbiz!' To which they say, 'I didn't mean it that way' and I know they didn't. But when I'm not recognised, and I wonder also about other Black celebrities who, when they aren't recognised and instead get stopped at the airport to be searched at customs, ignored in stores, served drinks last at the bar – do we have a feeling it's because we're Black? I understand the average Black person feeling that way, because that's what life has shown him; but it hasn't shown me that, from when I was young growing up in Jamaica, when I came to London or even today. But on the odd occasion it does happen, and I feel it.

I have had the discussion about being 'elevated out of Blackness' with my wife Andrea, who is white, and asked her about her perception of Black people she doesn't know. She didn't know me when I was John Barnes, the so-called superstar footballer for Liverpool, so I hope (no, I know!) she fell in love with me for who I am: John Barnes the person, who happens to be Black, not John Barnes the Liverpool footballer. I've asked her whether she saw all Black people like me. After making her feel very comfortable with her own truth and her understanding that the environment she came from influenced the way she viewed race, she acknowledged that she did see people differently, based on what she had been socialised to think. So, when she met me, and saw how 'normal' I was, she fell in love with me despite my colour. This is an unconscious/subconscious feeling we all have, and just as it gladdens me when I meet a Muslim Liverpool supporter with pictures to sign who reminds me about the danger of unconscious perception, I'm sure my wife now consciously thinks about her perception of others.

Andrea is white, as was my first wife, and there is a perception that Black men may marry white women in order to 'elevate their status' because they feel inferior. That certainly wasn't the case for me. I've had Black girlfriends in the past, but looking back, of those, did they look more like light-skinned Beyoncé or Tyra Banks, than dark-skinned Lupita Nyong'o or Alek

Wek? In terms of complexion and features, it was the former, because that is what we have always been taught and shown is the epitome of beauty. Why aren't thick lips, a broad nose, afro hair, a round face and jet-Black skin the standard of beauty to admire? Because that is what the quintessential 'African' looks like, so that isn't what beauty, morals or intellect look like. Because of this, Africans have been judged and divided along those lines for years.

Even growing up in Jamaica among Black people, we were taught unconsciously and subliminally to view lighter-skinned Jamaicans as superior, and if you could have a little 'good hair', even better. Like the concept of 'Americanness' being the epitome of greatness and not necessarily a nationality, 'whiteness' has taken on a new dimension of all things great, without the actual 'colour' being the main criteria.

Japanese women many years ago walked around with umbrellas in the summer, because they didn't want to get a tan as that gave the impression that they did manual labour outside and therefore were of a lower socio-economic status. White European women were considered more beautiful if they were pale skinned. Now times have changed: many white women want to tan themselves until they are darker than Black people, enlarge their lips and have bum implants for a curvier look. That's when they feel they look the most attractive. Many Black West African women are already dark, have full lips and naturally big bums. So, why aren't they considered by society as the most beautiful? Because they aren't white. And here I'm not talking about the colour, I'm talking about the idea of 'whiteness'.

FOR SOME BLACK PEOPLE, IT'S EASIER BEING WHITE

Why do some Black people lighten their skin? It causes anger and debate in the Black community, because they are perceived to be ashamed to be Black. We criticise them and say they have low self-esteem, but we don't analyse the reason behind that. On one hand, we reject and feel ashamed or embarrassed by the image of a dark Black person, then on the other we criticise people who try to not look like that. Just like in football where we analyse, criticise and dissect every mistake made by referees then at the end go on to say, 'but we must respect the officials'. This is how the idea of 'Blackness' – the race, not the colour – has developed a negative connotation in all our minds. Because why is a Black person who likes and wants lighter skin deemed to be ashamed of his or her race, while a white person can not only want darker skin, but also thicker lips and a bigger bum, yet they are not deemed to be ashamed of his or her race?

To a white woman who has an ordinary job and an average existence who wants to be a celebrity and craves bigger lips, a bigger bum and darker skin, if you said, 'You can have all that naturally in your next life, but you would have to become Black permanently' (the race, not the colour), I doubt she would accept that offer. Then propose the scenario where she is able to be the exact same person, from LA with a Hollywood mansion, be super rich, like the same music, have the same friends and family, look exactly as she wishes she looked now but she would have to be of the Black race. That sounds like a good deal given that she cares more about her looks and appearances than anything else and would be better off in every sense of the word but one. But that one fact supersedes everything else. It may be a ridiculous hypothesis, but think about it.

I know a lot of Black people who, given the choice, would rather come back as white in a future life. And it's not because they are ashamed to be Black; it's that they understand that for the average person it would afford them a better chance of being successful. Their life experiences have shown them that in the world we live in, it's easier being white. When you are forced to think about it honestly, you then consciously see the way the world reacts to people like you in relation to others and know that you are regarded differently, even if you're a Black celebrity who has been elevated out of Blackness. Because what are you when you are no longer a Black celebrity? Just Black.

The idea of 'colourism' is important when we consider our perceptions of worthiness, beauty and intelligence. Among Black people there are obviously a large variety of different skin shades and tones, and this can have a clear effect on such perceptions and the way some are treated in society. We argue that it's important for Black people to see other average Black people on TV because it gives us a sense of pride and hope that we can achieve our dreams, and that society is evolving and giving Black people opportunities. This is part of the thinking behind Black History Month. I view it differently. I think it's more important that white people see more Black people on TV, and are more aware of Black History Month, for them to see that Black people are just like them and are equally as ingenious, hardworking and worthy. Because to change the future, Black people don't need to change the perception of themselves; white society has to change its perception of Black people.

Do people look like monkeys or do monkeys look like people? Some do. Black, white or Asian, we are related to them. We all know someone who has a slight resemblance to an ape. Is that racist? Is calling a Black man 'ignorant' racist? Now I am fully aware the terrible reasons how and why these misconceptions of Black people came about, but why can't a Black man look like a monkey, like some white men do? Or be lazy and ignorant as some white, Chinese and Asian men are, without it being racist?

Empathy and understanding are the most important weapons in the fight for equality. What makes somebody strap a bomb to their body and walk into a restaurant and detonate it? Could we do that? Of course not, just like we couldn't kill our spouses in Rwanda. Are these people less than human, psychopathic or sociopathic with no feelings whatsoever? They must be. Were they not happy little children once upon a time, with loving parents who liked to play and laugh with their friends like the rest of us? Either they were, and something happened along the way to make them become the people they are, or they never were, which means they were born into an environment of hopelessness, despair and oppression, resulting in them being the people they are.

How lucky are we? If the roles were reversed, would we be any different? We would all like to think so, because we prefer to see ourselves like the stars and heroes of past Hollywood films who are benevolent, kind and compassionate. We would sacrifice ourselves before doing anything dishonourable. The problem with that is, 99 per cent of us think that is how we'd be, but only 1 per cent of us would actually be that way. I would like to think I would be in that 1 per cent, but maybe I wouldn't. We can never know until we are put in that particular situation.

So, what's the solution? What is it that makes someone want to strap a bomb to themselves, racially abuse someone or feel superior to others? It's not helpful to only treat the 'symptom', i.e. the actions 'blowing up yourself and others', 'throwing bananas at a Black footballer' or 'judging racial minorities as inferior'. The solution to most if not all problems, including the problem of racism, is to find out the cause or reason behind them.

HOW WE SEE THE WORLD

I like to use everyday examples – films, articles, television pro-grammes – to reflect the way the world is and how we become subliminally indoctrinated. We can also use these to show how the world should be.

Let's take as an example the TV talent shows, *The Voice* and *The X Factor*. On *The Voice* the judges close their eyes (or in this example, face the other way in the spinning chair) and listen to who sings better. They don't know what the person looks like, they don't have a preconceived perception of them, they just listen to the truth of their voice and make a judgement of their ability based on that. Conversely, on *The X Factor* the judges are facing the participants when they walk out, so not only do they have a preconceived perception of them, but they also know how the world will react to them based on their appearance. Before the participant even opens their mouth to sing, the judges know whether they shoot them to stardom, even if they're not that talented (unless they sound like screeching cats). From these examples, I'm sure you can tell which one is 'the way the world is' and which is 'the way the world should be'.

When you go for an interview, the interviewer should close their eyes, not even listen to accents or whether it's a male or female voice, but just listen to the intelligence of the person and make a decision. When Eric Cantona, with his French-accented English, spoke about seagulls following the trawler for scraps thrown overboard, he was a philosopher. If Paul Merson, with his cockney accent, said the same thing, they'd say he was an idiot. Ignore the accents – close your eyes and listen, then judge.

On the other end of the humanity scale, television provides a raw and brutal picture of how the world really is for those suffering intolerable discrimination. It is thought-provoking to see interviews with women from war-torn Middle Eastern or African countries, telling their stories of rape, murder and degradation. Often their husbands and children will have been brutally killed in front of them, however they speak in a way that may be perceived as 'lacking feelings', seeming very calm and matter of fact about their experiences. In some cases, they have become desensitised to the traumas they've experienced and are just accepting of their fate. They have come to under-stand that this has always been, and continues to be, the reality of their existence. They feel so hopeless, helpless and alone; human nature takes over as a defence mechanism to protect their psychological well-being, by flattening emotions so as to not be destroyed mentally by them. In nature, animals have an instinct for survival, they fight to preserve their lives. When you see a gazelle running from a cheetah, initially the desire to get away is evident, but once the cheetah fixes its jaws around the gazelle's throat, acceptance of its fate is then incredibly evi-dent in its eyes. When it's first caught, the gazelle may fight for a few seconds to escape, then you can see a physical relaxation, and lack of any fight, although it probably still has a minute before it dies. This is because it recognises the inevitability of the situation; its expression doesn't seem to be one of pain, discomfort or panic. And how sad is it, that we see the same reaction in certain human beings when going through the same hopelessness, or inevitability of a sad outcome.

I was watching Piers Morgan on *Good Morning Britain* speaking to Geoffrey Boycott, retired England cricketer, in the spring of 2021, during the national rollout of the Covid-19 vaccine. Despite already having been able to receive his first-dose vaccine due to his age, he then felt he deserved his second vaccine before some people had had their first. He was concerned that when the lockdown rules were eased a few months down the line, he would only be 52 per cent protected, not worrying about those others who would have no protection at all at that point. Piers agreed and said that as a 'national treasure' Boycott should be able to be afforded this privilege, Susanna Reid and Dr Hilary, however, were quick to shoot him down following this opinion. This is a good example of how many people in the UK have particular opinions and feelings about those who are deemed to be more worthy and deserving, once again demonstrating unconscious bias towards certain groups.

Candace Owens is a young, Black American Republican political commentator and TV host who shares many controversial opinions and is outspoken in her criticisms of the Black Lives Matter movement and Democratic Party. Alongside many other Black Republicans, she may be right in some of her provocative thoughts to a certain extent. One idea she takes issue with is the extent of benefits and financial aid provided for people of lower socioeconomic status. What she feels is, that in doing this, it can, for some, disincentivise people to strive for excellence. The problem is that many of these people are likely not enamoured or endowed with the dynamism it takes to become extremely successful entrepreneurs, businesspeople, doctors, celebrities; they are happy to lead a normal, 'average' lifestyle. So what happens to them? Should we not provide aid for anyone at all, in the hope that this will give them the push they need to create a high-flying successful life for themselves? This is not realistic for every single person. The same is true for all races, and the establishment has a responsibility to provide for all its citizens, not just its brilliant ones.

HOW THE WORLD TREATS US

What we all crave is a feeling of worthiness, acceptance and appreciation. Does that come from things we have actually done or achieved? Or does it come from the way the world sees us? Does Brad Pitt know he is attractive to women, or is it just the response that he gets from women that makes him feel that way? In a parallel world, if women or society never told him he was attractive, but he looked exactly as he does now, would he still think he was attractive? I have this discussion with my wife and her sister all the time about women who they think are attractive, particularly famous, talented women. I say to them, 'I bet if they worked down the road in McDonald's you wouldn't think they were so amazingly beautiful', which they deny. The same goes for attractive famous men. With regard to certain dynamics that you can't measure (e.g. worthiness, beauty, etc) the way we feel comes from however the world treats us.

In the 1992 FA Cup semi-final, while playing for Liverpool I thought I had scored the equaliser against Portsmouth but in the dressing room after the game I saw all the players instead praising Ronnie Whelan. I felt a bit slighted that I wasn't receiving any of those congratulations, but, even if I had scored, shouldn't the fact that we'd won have been enough for me? Why did I need the validation of others to feel more special? Because as human beings that's what we crave, and unfortunately some people get that validation every day without earning it.

An episode of the BBC programme *HARDTalk* featured author Bernardine Evaristo discussing winning the Booker Prize in 2019 for her novel *Girl, Woman, Other*. She talked about working within the establishment to try to change things with regard to race relations. Her book, which features principally Black women, has been well received because the way she has written about these characters has enabled everyone to empathise with them. However, if this book were to be made into a film it might be difficult for it to be as well received, and that is because of the continued negativity and lack of visual empathy towards Blackness in the mainstream media. No matter what emotional attachment people have towards the characters, be it love, sympathy, sorrow or empathy for their trials and tribulations, because of our historical indoctrination and what we are used to seeing, the Western audience would feel all these emotions more strongly when watching Gwyneth Paltrow or Anne Hathaway, rather than Black actors. Even with less well-known white actors, we will feel their pain, sorrow, joy or love more than we would for unknown Black actors. But in book form we create our own visual characters and even though the audience knows they are Black, they aren't necessarily actually seen as Black. That's when people can really say, 'I don't see colour', because they see them as whatever character they accept and are able to empathise with in their mind.

White society supports the white celebrity using what is sometimes considered their 'saviour image' in going to Africa and helping poor Black communities. Whether this is right or wrong, until Black celebrities can influence empathy themselves among white society or until sponsors are interested in giving money to organisations fronted by Black celebrities, then what else is the solution to getting aid to starving children? So, I'll keep on hoping that white celebrities continue using their influence to help regardless of their authenticity or integrity as its much needed until change is brought about. Black celebrities complain about this issue and feel they need more representation in that space but once again, if the sponsors and society at large aren't going to empathise with and support that image, who's to blame? The sponsors, or society?

We have to actually see colour, gender and sexuality first before we start to say we see their similarities to ourselves. It is wrong and dangerous to say we don't see these things. In doing so it negates the obvious important differences and renders them insignificant, but that shouldn't be the case. Those differences do exist and shouldn't be ignored as firstly, they can be an important part of a person's identity, and secondly, if something doesn't work out for someone from one of these groups be it professionally or personally, the 'difference' is used as the reason for failure. Whereas if we were to acknowledge and accept our differences, and following this recognise our similarities, then any perceived reason for the failure, of any situation, would be the same as it was for everyone. When white people say they don't see colour, they mean they see everyone as the same. But the same as who? As themselves. They think that this is a compliment, seeing a similarity between another person and themselves, and that makes them feel better about themselves/the situation. What they are actually doing, if that's true, is relegating the obvious difference (colour) to nothingness and insignificance in order for them to feel less guilty. If they were to see your colour then that would be insulting! But why should seeing colour be an insult? Isn't the negative perception that they fear they have, or would be interpreted to have, the real reason for 'not seeing colour'?

With regard to the argument of white people saying they don't have racial bias because they have some Black friends and see all of them as equal, it makes no sense even on a theoretical level. For their argument to hold up mathematically, each Black individual would need to have AT LEAST 50 per cent of the white population as individual allies (not just ONE individual white ally, which is their current argument). If the Black guy goes for a job interview, his 'white ally mathematics' argument will only help him if his particular white ally happens to be on the hiring panel for the job, which of course won't be the case. The hiring panel would be the millions of the rest of the white population who aren't his ally. And this is the case for every individual instance. So, if every white person knows and respects only 1 per cent of the Black population who may be their friend, then even if 100 per cent of white people have a few Black friends, every one of them still would see 99 per cent of Black people as different and unequal but are able to convince themselves otherwise. Now there's no technical name for disproving their argument; they're just mathematically incorrect.

The idea of equality doesn't exist. When white people say, 'We see ourselves just like you', to Black people, are they humbling themselves and inferring that they feel at the same level, a lower level, because of their innate sense of false humility? If they said, 'We see you (a Black person) just like us', that would mean they have elevated this Black person above the space they have unconsciously viewed Black people in for centuries. In reality though, that wouldn't be the truth. They are sincere with such a statement when talking about Black people who they know; friends, celebrities or people they consider to be intelligent, but not the average Black person. Just like the way that dynamic doesn't exist among white people regarding their perception of white working-class people, because the possibility of differences between them has nothing to do with colour, and again that's where the nuance of class comes in.

The Black/white dynamic when it comes to success and failure represents polar opposites. We individualise a Black man's success, but if he fails then we question the abilities of his whole group. And conversely, we individualise a white man's failure, but his group's ability wouldn't ever be questioned for his actions alone. Getting an intelligent Black person into a position of power won't mean that his ability will give anyone the opinion that there is a transactional benefit to having more Black people in similar positions, as they will individualise that person and 'elevate them out of Blackness'. So, until we change our perception of Black worthiness generally, not individually, nothing will change.

Class, race and politics are all intertwined. I was involved in a debate on Twitter surrounding an incident when Barack Obama disagreed with the President of Guinea over his comments stating that European/American colonialism negatively affected the progress of Africa. One man chipped into this Twitter debate asking me why I agreed with this and what made me think that I knew better than Obama. But the real question should have been, why does he think Obama knows more than the President of Guinea about his own country and continent? It is a demonstration of our unconscious bias towards Americans over Africans, even in the situation where both people are Black, because one is from the powerful West and is seen to have been elevated out of Blackness. Obama still represents Western capitalist values, so unconsciously won't be inclined to criticise America or the West too much.

ABUSE ON SOCIAL MEDIA

There is a lot of talk about trying to stop online abuse at the source. Now to me, this should actually mean getting to the source, i.e. the mind of the perpetrator, before it goes online and addressing why they feel this way. People who abuse others on social media are weak cowards who are looking for their lives to be deemed important and have meaning. By high-lighting, focusing on and replying to or engaging with their abuse we are actually empowering them to feel important. And even if we don't know who they are by name, they know that they are being spoken about which makes them feel relevant. If we instead ignored them and didn't give them power by discussion, they would likely soon crawl back into their little holes. On the other hand, though this could be an answer to reducing abuse online, it wouldn't address the issue of needing to re-educate these people on their wrongful prejudices and therefore doesn't actually get to the root of the problem.

Survival of the fittest in nature is a real concept. Its original meaning, for humans, animals and plants, was that whoever is best suited to their environment in terms of ability to acquire the things they need to survive, grow and reproduce will dominate. That dynamic continued for animals and plants, but for humans another layer was added. It became not just about doing what we need to survive, but about having MORE than we need to survive, to the detriment of other members of our species. Originally, different types of humans would go around colonising the world. Then came the idea of homo sapiens colonising the plant to the detriment of the other humanoid groups. Then the modern human overtook the world through 'class theory'. And finally came 'European colonisation' around the world using discrimination based on the lie of racial hierarchy, despite the fact many of these different 'races' had previously lived with each other for thousands of years. That concept has been the major distinguishing factor between humans and other members of the natural world, and has become our new 'natural state'. So, characteristics of who we now would consider to be the 'fittest' are based on lies. Once we re-establish a reality that isn't based on race, then we will have a much fairer representation of our perception of worthiness among all people. That's when the theory of survival of the fittest will go back to its original, more natural state.

HOW WE SEE EACH OTHER

I went for a walk the other day in my little village, strolling through a lovely area called the Dales which has beautiful views overlooking North Wales. It was afternoon time, when schools had just been let out; there were a few people walking their dogs and we were making small talk about what a lovely day it was. As I walked away, a young girl was also walking down the road right beside me; being a father of children around the same age, and with schools just re-opening again during the coronavirus pandemic, I struck up a conversation asking her if she was glad to be back at school. She answered politely, but I got the sense that she was uncomfortable talking to me and she started to shuffle about. I suddenly realised that she was nervous, and rather than be offended that she would dare to suggest that 'I' could in any way be a danger to 'her', I crossed the road and took a different route to make her feel more comfortable.

Similar situations have happened many times, when I've been walking late in the evening if I happen to be going in the same direction as a woman on her own. Now there is nothing more awkward than walking in the same direction, at virtually the same pace as someone (man or woman) for a distance. You feel as though you should say something while you're alongside them for those few minutes to break the awkwardness. When it happens to be a woman late at night, it's even more uncomfortable, because we are all aware of the reality of life, and we know how vulnerable women feel under those circumstances. In this situation, I try to speak in a cheerful way about something random to make them feel at ease and if they respond in a relaxed way, I may continue the conversation or not. But importantly, I recognise when they feel uncomfortable, and in this case I have no problem crossing the road, slowing down (or speeding up when I was younger and fitter!), or stopping to pretend to tie my shoelace so that they are well ahead of me and have no reason to feel threatened. That is ME doing something to change the situation, while others may say that the person feeling uncomfortable should be the one to do something. This goes for race also. People feel that they should not have to feel 'put out' by adapting their behaviour just because someone feels potentially threatened or vulnerable, because they know they are not a rapist or sexual abuser. But that doesn't stop that person feeling vulnerable, because of the experiences they have gone through during their life.

I was watching Ulrika Jonsson being interviewed on TV, and she said that every single one of her female friends has either been raped, abused, sexually assaulted, sexually harassed or sexually discriminated against. I know that to be true, and I believe her 100 per cent. Many don't. Similarly, every single one of my Black friends at some point in their lives has been racially abused or discriminated against, but we are not believed. The media, once again, pits different groups against each other with headlines such as, '10 YEARS FOR TEARING DOWN STATUES, BUT 5 YEARS FOR RAPE.' This inflammatory statement then causes some women to turn against the Black Lives Matter movement because they feel less supported. It's always the same: keep the marginalised groups separate, enemies even, as divided we are weaker. That's why I say once again, ALL disenfranchised groups should support and empathise with each other, and we must ignore the narrative influenced and promoted by the media of MY PROBLEMS ARE GREATER THAN YOURS!

6

WHICH BLACK LIVES MATTER?

George Floyd, a 46-year-old African American man, was murdered on 25 May 2020 by police officer Derek Chauvin who, during an arrest, knelt on his neck for 9 minutes and 29 seconds. This act was captured on camera in the streets of Minneapolis and quickly became a worldwide news story. What followed was a rise in visibility and acknowledgement of the Black Lives Matter movement around the world, with many marches, protests and calls for change in society.

I have thought in depth and for a long time about this incident, and what it really symbolises. Derek Chauvin, like most if not all people, is racially biased. We of course already know that, but is this dynamic the only thing that was taking place on that fateful day? No. His racial bias was the start for him to feel he could violently suppress Floyd and kneel on his neck,

139

acting with no regard for him as a human being. But, as the minutes ticked by, something else happened. It became about power and authority, and not just over George Floyd. Imagine the scenario where no onlookers were present; after Floyd was subdued and handcuffed, things would likely have subsided quicker, and Floyd might have survived. But instead, as the crowd gathered people started complaining, shouting and insisting that he take his knee off George Floyd's neck. Chauvin's power and authority were questioned and challenged, not by Floyd, but by the public who he also felt superior to and felt he knew 'better than'. The more they shouted, filmed and insisted that he do what THEY demanded, the more he became determined to continue with what he was doing. Because, in his mind, who were they to tell him what to do, he was more important than them?! We can simplify it as just a race issue and say that he wouldn't listen to a crowd of Black people shouting at him to stop and filming him, but there were also white people present in that crowd and he ignored them too. That's because he saw those white people in that less well-off area as inferior too. And these are the complexities of discrimination and shows the extent class comes into play.

Let's imagine the scenario in a different way: that the people telling Chauvin to take his knee off George Floyd's neck were people of high standing in society. While we assume that because Chauvin is racist, then he wouldn't listen to any Black person telling him to stop. But if for example, Barack Obama or Oprah Winfrey came out of the corner shop and shouted at him, he would listen. He would listen to Bill Gates or Jeff Bezos, or any white (and many Black) celebrities or prominent people. That is because he would consider those people to be at least his equal and would be happy to be subservient to them, even the Black ones. I feel that the fact that the people in those crowds were ones he saw as inferior, be they Black or white, is the reason he kept his knee on Floyd's neck for as long as he did.

The narrative of white police brutality towards Black people is interesting. A few years ago, I saw a fly-on-the-wall documentary from Sierra Leone about the police and how they caught criminals. Every policeman was Black, as was every criminal, and the police superintendent made no bones about their rough treatment of the accused and how they regularly had to beat a confession out of them. Groups of young boys were rounded up, the working-class kids of the capital, who were well known to be so. On one occasion, a lower-ranked policeman rounded on a group of unknown youths and was severely reprimanded by the superintendent . . . because they could have been sons of known people in prominent positions! So these were the WRONG PEOPLE (i.e. sons of politicians, doctors, lawyers and such like); while they were ALL Black, there were some Black people who were considered to be more worthy of our respect and empathy. In other words, class is also a major factor in this situation.

In times of stress and confrontation, we can all be guilty of exerting our perceived superiority over anyone we consider inferior to us. Here is a simple example: as a father, I might insist on my child doing something, going to bed at a certain time for instance. It's not important whether I'm right or wrong but I'm the parent, so I insist. If my child complies, that's fine. If they moan a little but still do it, that's fine. If they argue their point, but then still do it, that too is fine. If they continue to argue and, through their incessant argument, prove to any rational person (myself included) that what they want to do actually makes more sense, then the battle becomes not a question of who is right or wrong, but of whether they have the power and authority to override my decision, no matter how ridiculous that decision may be. I have been in this situation many times and have ended up making them do what I say, even if they were right. Now if my wife, who I consider to be my equal (and superior at times) gets involved and tells me

EXACTLY what the children have been telling me, then I may then climb down, change my stance and convince myself that that decision instead could be reasonable, but only because their mother insisted.

The Black Lives Matter story really shook the world in 2020, but the origins of this movement came years before in the wake of the murder of seventeen-year-old Trayvon Martin, who was shot by George Zimmerman in Florida. Similar to the Me Too movement – which was founded in 2006 by Tarana Burke, an African American female, and subsequently made more famous many years later when white American actresses began to quote the movement – the agenda was then picked up and run with by different groups of people to promote their own agenda. Talk about conflation: every man and his dog then adopted the BLM slogan to conduct whatever he deemed necessary to make his or her point, which at times had nothing to do with the real issue of Black lives actually mattering. Not more than anyone else, not less than – just mattering.

There was push back and objection to the terminology, because of course 'all lives matter'. While there has never been a need to push the narrative that white lives matter, as soon as the Black Lives Matter term became fashionable, naysayers started to then give examples of poor, struggling, working-class white people and moaning that their lives mattered as well! Funny that they weren't too concerned about those poor white lives before. This is where the nuances of race and class discrimination becomes apparent again, as we discussed earlier. While everyone knows that all lives do matter of course, there is a dynamic that is in need of more urgent action for change, that disproportionately affects certain groups in a much more negative and destructive way and this needs to be addressed first.

This concept is similar to when the Black elite focus on and highlight racism in sport, music and film and try to come up with a plan of action to combat this. When it is pointed out to them that actually there is a huge need to tackle inequality in the inner-city communities regarding jobs, education, housing, social services, knife crime, the response is always a simple, superficial, 'Well, we have to do both.'

When we focus on high-profile incidents of racial injustice and hang our hats on that narrative to try to make society not only feel guilty, because its 'their' community that is persecuting us, but to also accept culpability for its actions, we begin to see some defensive push back and quotations around the number of Black people who are actually killed, robbed or exploited by 'their own', i.e. other Black people. That's when the 'statistics' and 'data obsessed' people come out of the woodworks – oh, don't get them wrong, they are still supporting us, but they're 'just saying . . .'

When we see reports stating there are more Black people attacked by other Black people in Black American communities or Black African countries compared to white on Black crime, people will say, 'So why do you say this is a problem to do with racism in our communities?' You may argue that they have a point, but the dynamics in those situations have nothing to do with race; this is where socio-economic issues, political beliefs and class often determine the reasons behind the crime. We need to stop giving the 'whatabouters' an opportunity to push back and to do this we have to adopt a different focus on 'which Black lives matter'. We must focus on the victims, rather than the perpetrators, because as they may point out, in many cases the perpetrators are Black people themselves – this gives white society a get out clause. So, the Black lives that 'don't seem to matter' are the vast majority who have been killed by other Black people, by 'their own'. In that situation, it's not a race crime, so does it not matter as much? We forget about those lives; the lives of those who struggle to get jobs, housing, an education, access to social services and therefore live among communities where crime rates are high, and they may be exploited by 'their own people' – well, those Black lives matter to me too.

It seems to me that the only Black lives that matter, if we are to believe the media, are the ones who have been killed by white policemen, the ones who can't win an Emmy or an Oscar or the ones who receive racial abuse from a fan at a football match. The extreme epitome of this issue to me, an example which was mind-blowingly swept under the rug for people to forget about, is the 400 schoolgirls who were abducted from their school in Nigeria by Boko Haram in 2014, never to be seen or heard of again (except the few that in recent years have managed to escape). Had they been blonde-haired, blue-eyed school-girls taken from a school in Stockholm, you can imagine the drastically different world response.

FRANCE AND ENGLAND

The most interesting thing about the solution to inequality is the difference between the two biggest beneficiaries of colonial-ism, France and England. In France, there is a larger population of Black people than in England, but as Black people over here we seem to have not only more power and bigger platforms to voice our concerns, but a much larger presence in the higher echelons of society. That's because the philosophy (real or imagined) of these two countries is completely different, and both disingenuous I might add. In France, ever since the French Revolution, in the late 1790s, there has been the idea that your loyalty and identity with FRANCE itself supersedes race and religion. So, ALL citizens, regardless of ethnicity or religion, are supposed to be treated equally. Therefore, all the minorities are technically 'just French' and supposedly there can be no discrimination as everyone belongs to this same group. Whether this is the reality is another question, one that we all know the answer to.

In Britain, however, Black people have a much larger voice and do seemingly climb higher up the ladder than Black people in France in greater numbers. Here we do accept the differences of British people and acknowledge the fact that some British people (i.e. those from different ethnicities or religions) are discriminated against and seen, even in the eyes of the law, as different. The reality is that all we accomplish in doing so is to place more elite Black people into higher positions of power. Despite the differences in these two societies, in both countries the vast majority of Black people, those who are everyday working-class people, actually remain disenfranchised and exploited.

There are layers to discrimination, gender, race, class, etc., and we have to try to strip as many of those layers away. If as Black people, we say, 'Let's strip the race layer away', we should actually try to strip away the layer of perceived 'Black inferiority' and not 'Black individual' discrimination, as is the same towards gender or class.

Journalist Darren Lewis featured on *Good Morning Britain* discussing the Black Lives Matter movement. He talked about the fact that there are no Black board members of the FA, not one Black Premier League referee and he also mentioned police brutality, lack of education, poor housing, 'stop and search' within the Black community and said all of these issues are what the BLM movement is trying to tackle. Richard Madeley, *Good Morning Britain* host, was left open-mouthed, appalled. 'You mean there really isn't one Black board member of the FA, and no referees?! Something needs to be done!', he demanded. Nothing was mentioned about police brutality, education or those other increasingly important and devastating issues to the wider Black community. This is unconscious bias at its most obvious: knowing that there are elite Black people deserving of more, but not even thinking about those non-elite Black people who are forgotten about and left behind in poverty. This is not a criticism of Richard in this scenario at all; he is not unique in his unconscious bias. This is to highlight that our concerns for equality of Black people in elite positions seem to be a priority and the ambivalence towards the average non-elite Black person is in us all.

7

ELEVATED OUT OF BLACKNESS

It amazes me when people only cry 'discrimination' when it affects them. Famous female actresses and businesswomen, famous Black footballers, famous gay sportspersons, famous disabled actors, famous white English football managers. What they/we all have in common is that to a certain extent we belong to the higher socio-economic echelons of society and therefore have a voice, and demand 'equality'. Who do we call on to support and get behind our cause? We call on the average voiceless people because we feel that by obtaining opportunities for ourselves, we will somehow be helping them. We are going about it the wrong way around, because all of those famous groups of people I mentioned above have been 'elevated out of' the perception of the group they belong to, in order to be worthy of their success. If they were to become seen as 'equal' it wouldn't be their 'group' becoming more equal, it would be for them as an 'individual'.

So, Meryl Streep and Helen Mirren winning Oscars means that only Helen Mirren and Meryl Streep are being given more opportunities, not 'all' actresses over sixty-five. Denzel Washington being given an Oscar means Denzel Washington is becoming equal to his white male counterparts. Karren Brady being accepted in the boardroom doesn't mean 'all' women are being accepted, or even 'more' women, just 'her'.

Instead, as celebrity champions of equality, when we feel we are discriminated against we should shout from the rooftops not about ourselves and how terrible our world is, but about our 'average' compatriot of the same group. Because until that 'average' person is accepted, while certain 'individuals' belonging to that group may be invited to sit at the top table with you know who, the group we belong to will never be accepted – and what do we want, equality for ALL or just OURSELVES?

The saddest thing for me, is when the average Black person feels sorry for me and other Black celebrities who they feel are being discriminated against. They may go on marches and protests complaining about the lack of opportunities for their Black heroes. That is why I call upon all the Black celebrities not to complain about lack of opportunities for themselves, or people like them (other celebrities), but rather to speak for the voiceless millions who support us but have no voice regarding their own existence and aspirations. And the only way to truly achieve equality is not for the 'greatest' of us to be accepted, but for the 'lowest' of us.

How passionately does the average Black person speak when demanding sanctions against an Eastern European team for racially abusing Yaya Toure. Why don't they make the same passionate demands to the government to improve the conditions and opportunities for themselves and their children? Is it because they feel nothing will change for them, so let's at least demand change for a few of us?

It's the same in America with the Black Lives Matter movement. Does a Black life only matter when it's taken by a white policeman? What about the many more Black lives that have been taken in their own communities? This is not me criticising Black on Black crime, this is me criticising the organisations for not marching, protesting, demanding the important changes educationally, socially and opportunity-wise in the inner cities of America for their children. Do they also feel hopeless and that there is no point, because no one of influence really cares and nothing will be done, so let's demand instead just a few white policemen be prosecuted when a case goes viral worldwide?

WHO IS THE REAL ENEMY?

People are happy to give in to certain meaningless demands, for example the 'Rooney Rule' in sport (an NFL policy requiring league teams to interview ethnic-minority candidates for head coach and senior jobs) to show progress towards racial equality. They are happy for some to be 'elevated out of Blackness', for a few policemen to be prosecuted and for a commentator who said a Black American footballer 'ran like a monkey' to be banned. The Rooney Rule may be necessary, but I'd rather be given the job or interview by merit. If we say, 'Well, that won't happen, therefore the Rooney Rule is the only way', we are giving up on things changing. And if we say, 'Give it time, because we aren't there yet', that will only delay us getting there. We won't have to challenge society to change, as such policies will give the illusion of progress. This rule first came about because there were only three or four Black head coaches in the NFL. Here we are twenty-odd years later and we are in the same position.

When Colin Kaepernick knelt during the playing of the anthem in support of the wider Black community and their struggle for justice and equality, it was done to highlight the problem of racial injustice in mainstream society and the unfair treatment of Black people. This has now been distorted into a discussion about NFL stars, and their right to freedom of expression, while the original message seems to have disappeared. Similarly, when Raheem Sterling spoke about the media's influence in creating the perception of Black people generally, that became distorted into, 'Let's support Raheem and other Black football players.' So, while it always starts out as a Black superstar sportsperson speaking out in support of the Black community, it turns into the Black community supporting Black superstars in their fight to protest.

Once again, the hierarchy is quite happy for this to happen, because it deflects and changes the focus from what is really important and a much more uncomfortable narrative: the disenfranchisement of Black society. So instead, we focus on the right of Black millionaires to 'take a knee' (What for? We may forget, but they have the right.) The establishment will encourage the average Black person to campaign for John Barnes, or other Black 'celebrities', to be given more opportunities, even for the prosecution of racist policemen, as long as they don't start demanding real tangible change for themselves and their communities. Because that would require looking at themselves, rather than pointing the finger at a few who happened to have been caught, and absolving themselves of responsibility.

I attended a Downing Street forum a few years back, and was able to have a discussion with David Cameron, in response to racism in football. When I mentioned the fact that there must be a holistic approach to racism in general, not just condemning Luis Suárez or John Terry or fans who racially abused a Black player, his response was 'that fight was for a different time', this was about banning, and condemning the ones found to be guilty. The more important message about 'justice for all' was lost for the more popular one of 'justice for the famous few'.

There are lots of privileged Black people starting committees, demanding funding and trying to help themselves get higher up the ladder. They will convince the wider Black community to support them, on the premise that their personal success will help Black communities in the long run. History has shown time and again, from the Magna Carta to the American Revolution, French Revolution, American Civil War, and countless others, that the privileged are usually interested in helping themselves, while convincing the 'masses' that its good for them.

A Black journalist wrote, 'Football players have had enough and are mobilising, and the wider Black community are rooting for them!' Remember how the French Revolution turned out for the very same 'masses' after the privileged few convinced them that it was for their benefit? That is why, recognising that I am one of the privileged few, I can't look myself in the mirror and go authentically to the masses asking them to get behind my fight to be a football manager, or whatever else I feel I'm being denied the opportunity to do, and try to convince them that it's also in their interest that I achieve this goal.

The industry where Black people are given the most tangible, equal opportunity is the sporting industry. Within in it, privileges are in abundance financially and socially (not with-standing racist abuse from the terraces) but when you are finished with the sport, because you can't compete anymore, the sport generally finishes with you in terms of other oppor-tunities the industry has to offer. For some reason, the focus on racial inequality is thrust on this industry more than any other, followed closely by the music, acting and media indus-tries, where we are fairly well represented and rewarded, while ignoring the place where the fight is much more necessary. This place is the wider average Black community.

EQUAL BUT DIFFERENT

Exploitation of the working-class masses, Black or white, is not only a feature but is a necessary trait in an elite capitalist society: the more people we can disenfranchise and exploit, the more success the system can achieve. The former colonies have shown this in the exploitation of their own people, so why do we feel as Black people in the UK and the US that if we had more power things would automatically be better for the Black working-classes? It doesn't work that way.

The idea of changing from within never works. You can easily become part of the system, and while your intentions may have been to make a difference, you may just wait for someone else later down the line to make a real difference while fooling yourself that you tried your best.

It's harder to stand up against something that's wrong than to stand up for something that's right. That's why communists say total revolution is the only way for change, as even revolutionaries joining an existing system won't change anything.

I don't want a socialist revolution, just a balance in providing MORE and not necessarily EQUAL for the masses. How the elite has always got away with promoting equality, without real equality actually happening, is the 'equal but different theory'. They get 100 per cent of what is due to 'them'. But that sum will not be the same for everyone. For example, two people doing the same job will get 100 per cent of their own worth, but one's worth may be seen as more than the other's. So, one could get £200 a week and the other £100 a week for the same job; for both that would be 100 per cent of what they 'deserve', as was the case throughout colonial times when white Europeans worked in the colonies and were paid more than their colonial colleagues for doing the same job. So, who is more deserving?

We talk about the demand for more Black representation in the higher echelons of society and businesses, but does the Black community, and the areas in which they live, then receive that same support from those businesses? Take the example of a Black McDonald's franchise that opened up in a poor, Black area. Rather than using their clout to campaign for improvements in that area, they complained about being placed in an underprivileged and less affluent location as they were concerned that they wouldn't be able to make as much money.

Even more surprisingly, these complaints were supported by that same Black community who would be satisfied with seeing a Black man being successful even it meant no improvements for themselves and where they live. We continue to see this with the community's support of 'X Black footballer' trying to be a manager, 'Y Black actor' winning an Oscar, etc. Just more examples of an elite group of people wanting to be elevated out of their communities rather than improving those areas.

White society has convinced the world that racists are the lowest of the low who abuse Black people. In reality, it's actually the elite who created racism, convincing the lower-class members of society that the reason for their discontent is the 'immigrant', instilling in them a racial bias, then punishing them for the racial discrimination that they created. If Black people need an example of an unrealistic utopia of racial support, all they need do is look at white society and see that so many average working-class white people are disenfranchised by the white elite. So why would the Black elite not do the same towards other so-called lesser members of the Black community? We see this happening in many African and Caribbean countries who are ruled by a Black elite. The white elite used the masses to make themselves richer by getting them to support their efforts in colonisation, while neglecting the needs of the working-class, feeding them scraps and convincing them they will benefit from having a stronger economy/nation. When in reality the majority of those individual people didn't benefit at all. Now we see a similar thing, with the Black elite telling Black people to own our own shit, spend money on Black businesses etc. White society has been doing that for years; the only ones to benefit remain the elite. We as Black people want equality, respect and to be seen as the same as white people, morally and intellectually, so why would we be different to them when it comes to this?

At the outset of any revolution, I'm sure the white non-elites of the time were of the same mindset as the Black non-elites of today in hoping, expecting and demanding representation as they felt that it would benefit them in the long run. But as hundreds of years have gone by, they've come to not only realise, but expect nothing to change. So, when their once upon-a-time-working-class heroes (Lord Alan Sugar, for example) succeed, they don't necessarily cheer and champion their rise as they know that won't make an iota of difference to the 90 per cent of the rest of their working-class people.

We are in a modern racial revolution, as I call it. In the last 150 years or so there have been a few of these, without much deep-rooted change. But particularly at this time, we are naïvely expectant of tangible change for all. History should be an example that if we carry on in the way we are, nothing will change apart from a few more Black people becoming elite. There have been many clues over the years, when we have seen elite Black, female, gay and other disenfranchised people alongside the old established order doing very nicely thank you very much, while the majority of their group struggle. But we, as Black people, have expected things to be different for US because of an illusion of BLACK TOGETHERNESS overcoming ELITISM. Why do we believe that we are morally superior and united as a race that we will be any different to those other groups of the past?

THE 'HAVES' AND 'HAVE-NOTS'

Unfortunately, if we were to look at society in 200 years' time, I fear we'd find that the Black experience then would look similar to the current day working-class experience where you have white 'haves' and white 'have-nots', Black 'haves' and Black 'have-nots', and all other groups separated by the 'haves' and 'have-nots'. There would be an acceptance of the way things are without the 'have-nots' hoping, demanding and expecting a hand from someone who was once upon a time just like them. Sadly, we are well on the way to that! The fight for equal opportunity will never be achieved because we can't escape the greed of humans, even the ones with the right intentions from the outset. To keep fighting in a binary way, meaning equality or nothing, is not only wishful thinking, but unfortunately unachievable in our lifetime. So, let's start with a more balanced expectation both in terms of what we can, and want to achieve. That is, understanding that there will always be the haves and the have-nots, both of different races, sexes, geographically, members of single parent families, travellers, socialists, communists, Muslims, Christians, the list goes on. But let's try to give the have-nots a little bit more of the pie to make life a bit fairer.

The majority of white working-class people will experience a chronic, dull pain in their lives from the difficulties they face due to their degree of societal disadvantage to which they are now accustomed and accept probably won't change. Black people, however, experience a sharp, excruciating pain, because we believe it will get better and struggle to just accept and endure it. Human beings' adaptability, perseverance and survival instinct allow us to endure most things and once we get used to certain situations, they become bearable. The Black community is not at that place yet, as we are hopeful things will get better, so we continue to feel the pain of the present. Unfortunately, if the present social and political environment we live in remains the same then things will never change, and if that's the case then just like white working-class people we would have to get used to the dull pain of acceptance.

While certain Black individuals will become pain free (as will certain individuals belonging to other disenfranchised and marginalised groups), there will still be those elite who claim their lives are terrible because of depression, abuse or discrimination. The society we live in today worships money, celebrity, prestige and fame, and puts these things as the real markers of success. So, how can people who achieve all of this go on to ask poor working-class people to empathise with any struggle they may be going through, despite the fact it appears they have all the ingredients needed for happiness? It's difficult for those working-class people to find empathy there. I believe that's one of the reasons behind why many white working-class people are not allies of Black people in the fight against racial inequality: because the focus is on the problems that Black CELEBRITIES and ELITES have, rather than your average Black person. Asking the white working-class to empathise with people who they consider have more than them in terms of success, and who moan about things that may seem trivial in the pursuit of happiness, is often met with resistance. It is the same reason that many white people reject the concept of white privilege: telling a poor white person that they are privileged, when they can't afford to feed their kids, get a better job or good housing, makes little sense to them. In their opinion, the underprivilege and struggles they face, negate any privilege that being white affords them. In order to gain this community as allies, we need to use examples of the experiences of Black non-elite people and the everyday struggles they go through. Maybe they would then have more empathy for those kinds of situations and be open to learning about and supporting the issues.

RACE AND CLASS

I have spoken a little about the nuances of race and class being intertwined in the discrimination dynamic; this is a common theme today among some white people who push back against the idea of racial discrimination. Often, they will point out the fact that in some cases, poor, white working-class people are worse off than working-class Black people. That's where we, as Black people, have to understand the history of class bias: the outcome for those societies of people within the same race, and the exploitation and disenfranchisement of the lower classes to create the inequities in society.

Going back hundreds if not thousands of years before the transatlantic slave trade, exploitation of the working class by the elite had always occurred, be it in feudal times in England in the eleventh century, or subsequent years when the elite controlled all wealth, and the lower classes would toil day and night increasing that wealth for them. During those times there was no question of unfairness or that people deserved to instead live equally; that was just the way it was.

But as time went on, certain people (the up and coming middle-class) began to crave more wealth and power from the aristocracy. They would revolt and pose the idea of 'more for the people!' to really just gain more for themselves, using the unhappiness of the wider population as a reason to threaten the establishment with uprising in order to make changes to the status quo. However, all that they changed was their own circumstance while nothing really changed for the rest of poorer society. This idea was seen through countless people's revolutions, from the Magna Carta to the French Revolution and the American War of Independence. Truly, this ideology was never about more wealth/power/decision-making opportunities for the masses, but only to bestow those privileges to a few of the newly endowed middle-class people.

Here we are, many years later, and nothing much has changed for the working class despite what people say. They may use examples such as the fact there are now indoor toilets and good sanitation for all in the UK which may not have been the case a mere seventy years ago. But, looking at the wider natural social and technological evolution which has occurred in that time, this alone is not a luxury to gauge improvement in the standard of living for the working class. Now, in the UK more than the US, we see a relatively new 'Black elite' who are demanding change and using the Black wider masses as the reason behind their fight. Sound familiar? We have already seen some of us elevated into positions of power, become the moral guardians for the establishment, criticise and punish a few scapegoats, make our influence stronger and pockets richer, while nothing really changes for the other 90 per cent of the Black community.

Many of the white working-class have accepted their fate (not individually, but collectively) in as much as they have become used to 'the way things are'. But the Black community generally hasn't, because of recent limited progress we have seen which gives us hope for a better tomorrow for all. Why should things be different for Black people in the West, than it was/is for white, Indian, Chinese, African or Caribbean working-class people all over the world who have been exploited by their own elite (within their own race). I'm sure the disenfranchised people of those groups felt the same as we do now at the outset of their class revolution hundreds of years ago.

We have the benefit of history to show us what the future looks like if we try to do things the exact same way they were done before. Do we think we are morally superior to those other groups of the past, to feel that we want to help our Black brothers and sisters to create true equality for all, or will we do what humanity has done for thousands of years and just create more elite people to reap the benefits and leave the remaining 90 per cent with no change at all?

It would make sense for the white working-class community to empathise with Black people, Muslims and other disen-franchised groups as they are all in the same boat – exploited by the elite. But this is not always the case. Why is it that often the most overt, obvious forms of racism we see comes from white working-class people? Looking back to the '60s when many people of different races came to the UK and lived among the white working-class, some of them did better financially by doing jobs that may have seemed undesirable to British working-class people who were not inclined to take those jobs. You would hear stories back then of Black people 'stealing jobs on buses'; fast forward to today where people tell stories of Eastern European people 'stealing OUR jobs', and it's clear to see how propaganda can convince the masses that the reason for their discontent is the inferior foreigner. The feeling of discontent and anger towards these groups was of course unconscious because of how people were conditioned to think ever since the British Empire gathered pace between the 1850s and 1940s. To see these people of different races who they had been indoctrinated to think of as 'inferior' now doing jobs alongside them, working as equals, was hard to take.

With this rise of the Empire, while Britain got richer the working-class stayed the same. So, to stop this community questioning the elite as to why this was the case, new narratives were created to explain their lack of financial progression. The new immigrant (Middle Eastern and Eastern European refugees) created another reason to blame for the inequalities among the white working-class people. First, it was the idea of menial jobs 'stolen' by the Caribbeans and Africans in the '60s and '70s. Then more migrant workers 'stealing' from semi-skilled jobs in the '80s and '90s. Now refugees 'stealing' benefits in the twenty-first century. You'll notice that the narrative is never about the foreign group reducing access to good education, better housing or economic equality which would reduce the gap between rich and poor – just the lesser beneficial opportunities, those that this community has been accustomed to for hundreds of years. Those that they have been led to believe is all that there can be for them. In order to avoid uprising and revolution against the elite, their perceived ceiling of opportunity for progression and wealth has been purposefully kept very low.

The vicious cycle of pitting groups of white working-class people against the Black community has taken a new turn. Working-class people are now being targeted as the main perpetrators for racial hatred and being punished for it. Those judging them are the newly created 'Black elite' who work among institutions to deliver 'educational programmes concerning racial rights and wrongs'. Because of this, the TRUE elite (white British leaders) avoid being criticised or blamed; they have appointed certain Black people to write the 'rule book' and as long as this rule book doesn't do anything to impact the status quo or challenge the establishment for real change then they're happy.

The reality is, these individual cases of racism that get blown up in the media have no impact whatsoever on the widespread racial inequalities suffered by 90 per cent of the Black community. But the Black elite have to be seen to be doing something: they focus, debate and highlight these petty incidents alongside the 'Black people have been slaves for too long' narrative which then shuts down any meaningful dialogue and ignores the real inequalities supported by the very institutions that fund and employ them. They fear going deeper into this topic and questioning the actions and responsibilities of their white leaders and those in charge, in case of losing their membership to the elite club. It's much easier to blame one single poor working-class football 'hooligan'.

The Black community, with the benefit of hindsight, have an opportunity to adopt a different approach to the question of true equality for all. But, at present, we are not taking that opportunity. We are allowing our Black elite to convince us (just as the white elite did to their wider communities hundreds of years ago) that the solution to the problem is to build them as individuals up, give them power and status, and subsequently things will change for the masses. Deep down we know that this is not the answer; we need to change our strategy.

THE ELITE/NON-ELITE DYNAMIC

Increasingly, I've started to look at the elite and non-elite dynamic, as I like to call it, rather than race, class, gender, etc. Why? Because, although throughout history there has been discrimination against people more generally, based on the above-mentioned dynamics, there has always also been individual members of those disenfranchised groups who have been part of a privileged elite. Now with the racial revolution, I was hoping that we would look to include everyone in our fight for equality, but it seems that we are following the thousand-year-old trend of just wanting more semi-elite people from our own group to become equal.

The European Super League in football is an extreme example of why you can't change things from within an existing system to benefit yourselves more than others. The most powerful clubs in Europe, Real Madrid, Juventus, Liverpool, Manchester United, etc., know that if they want to have more of a share of the profits in football they have to break away from UEFA and the existing structure to be able to get more for themselves. So why do we as Black people, who have far less power within most institutions than those huge clubs have within theirs, feel that all we have to do is to get a few of our elite members into the system and things will change for ourselves as a group?

There will always be push back against the argument that class, race or gender is a barrier to equality or success, by using examples of one or two successful individuals from each of those groups. We have an elite vs non-elite comparison which covers the whole demographic landscape of humanity, and that's what we have to address: closing the gap between rich and poor. The idea of racial hierarchy over the last 400 years, just gave the elite more people to legitimately exploit, while having to allow a few of those disenfranchised races into their elite club.

There will always be inequities between elites and non-elites, and the more we can debunk the idea of 'worthiness' based on class, gender, religion or race then the better the world will be. Those inequities are unfortunate, but factors such as geography, timing, place of birth, etc. also contribute to the wealth, happiness, acceptance and perception of worthiness towards the different groups of people. If we can get rid of the lies of racial hierarchy then at least we address one factor, but should we not be doing that hand in hand with addressing those other factors too?

Class plays as big a part in discrimination as race, and we as Black people have the benefit of history to show us this. We are trying to be accepted as equal by 'elevating' ourselves out of the image of the 'lower-class Black person'. We have seen Lord Alan Sugar, and thousands more working-class white men, elevate themselves out of their original 'class' and become extremely successful, but for one individual to achieve this, it has no effect on the negative perception of their original group still being seen as inferior. Now armed with this knowledge, why do we assume that getting more Black working-class people into higher positions of power will change the mainstream perception of our group or help the average Black person?

Class discrimination among Black people in Africa and the Caribbean, to a certain extent, has been around for over a hundred years; there has always been a Black elite in those places so there is an established acceptance of that dynamic. But in 'white countries' the vast majority, if not all, of the immigrant Black community are usually not only the working class of their adopted countries, but also were the working class of their original countries from where they emigrated. So, fifty years later, now their children are trying to do better than their parents did by elevating themselves up the class ladder. But as

I explained with regard to the white working-class people who did the same hundreds of years ago, or the Black elite in colonised countries who did something similar, the answer to the solution for equality in 'white countries' isn't to elevate more Black people into positions of power but to change the perception of the so-called lower classes. Otherwise, the 90 per cent of people who aren't able to 'elevate' themselves will be doomed to be just like the poor, disenfranchised white working-class in those countries, or the poor Black working-class in 'Black countries'.

Looking at the white community in general, from those living in poverty right up to the elite upper classes, it is clear to see there are inequalities, discrimination and differences in levels of respect among everyone belonging to that community. That simple fact encapsulates the whole problem that we face in trying to achieve racial equality and equal opportunities. With regard to the white community, until they treat each other as equal, how or why are they going to treat others so? And why do we as Black people expect that to happen?

I participated in a radio discussion with a very intellectual man on the subject of racism. I made the point that the real discrimination we have to tackle is the lack of opportunities – educational, social and economic – in the inner cities, particularly in the areas mainly occupied by Black people. He proceeded to quote Karl Marx and said that discrimination against the 'masses' has always been a problem. When I pointed out that Marx's comments would not have taken into consideration the added dynamic of 'race' compounding the problem, he dismissed it as if to say it's all the same for the working class. Following this, we spoke about the role that the media plays in influencing the public. I mentioned the issue of the narrative of 'Muslim terrorists', as opposed to that of 'lone wolf nutter' if the murderer happened to be white. His response was that this is how they 'self-identify'. Firstly, even if subsequent to an incident involving a Muslim, the perpetrator comes out and says they self-identify as a 'Muslim terrorist' claiming responsibility on behalf of some ideology; my point was that our initial perception, well before that happens, is that he is a terrorist. Why can't he just be a 'lone wolf nutter'? And secondly, when has it ever happened that a white person who has committed a similar terrorist offence then self-identifies as a 'lone wolf nutter' earning him that title in the media?

A huge problem we face is that many people think that all types of discrimination are the same. If white working-class people can work their way out of their depressed socio-economic situations, why can't Black working-class people do the same?

Race is just an excuse. What they fail to realise is, that for a lot of Black people who have worked their way up, they have done so despite being Black. For any white working-class person who has worked their way up, 'race' hasn't played any role in being a barrier to them achieving their goal. It hasn't necessarily helped them, but what they've been judged on, is their ABILITY. That is why I've said that some Black people have been successful DESPITE being Black; because they were also judged on their ABILITY, despite the negative perception people already have of them because they are Black.

Now, I know this sounds like a socialist manifesto, but it isn't meant to be. Because of people's individual greed (myself included), that dream of equality for all, no matter how idealistic it may be, is impossible to achieve, as China and Russia have shown us. However, a better balance between the 'haves' and the 'have-nots' can be attainable if we learn from the mistakes of the past.

8

DISCRIMINATON:
OTHER MARGINALISED GROUPS

For the last few years, I have tried to widen any debate on racial bias that I'm involved in, to include general discrimination against different disenfranchised groups (women, LGBTQ community, Muslims, trans people, etc.). In doing so, I am regularly told that I'm 'conflating' the issue and should just keep it to one particular subject. I disagree with this, because not only is the principle of the nature of the bias the same, i.e. how we have been wrongly conditioned to think about the worth of any of those particular groups in relation to the dominant group, but the solution lies in the empathy, acceptance and examination of all of these groups 'together'.

If you were to ask some Black men what they think about discrimination towards women, they may not be particularly interested because it doesn't negatively affect them. If you were to ask some white women about discrimination towards Black men, they may not be that interested, as again, it also doesn't negatively affect them. And the same could be said for straight men's opinions on discrimination towards gay men, etc. I could go on. The point being, from a race perspective (you can also adopt the same rationale to the other dynamics) why should white society care about racial equality towards Black people when they are not negatively affected by it? In fact, often they benefit more from that inequality. And secondly, why should Black people expect white society to care, when some of us ourselves don't consider the discrimination towards other groups?

SEXISM IN SPORT

Karren Brady, CEO of West Ham United – young, attractive, highly intelligent and undoubtedly competent – goes into the boardroom of another Premier League club, and how is she made to feel? I suppose it's not too bad now, as the composition of the boardroom of football clubs has changed and has younger, more dynamic businessmen who, in their lives before football, likely dealt with women at various levels within their particular industry. So, let's go back ten to fifteen years when she first started out. How do you think the old codgers in the boardroom would have perceived her position, being so high up in a football club? I'm 100 per cent sure she would tell you that she felt that a lot of them were very condescending, and acted like she shouldn't be in that position because she didn't have the expertise or knowledge to be there. Once again, and I'll keep on saying it, this perception ISN'T PERSONAL!

It's likely that Karren would have felt that that their conde-scension and lack of respect was an attack on her competence personally, but it wouldn't have been. Just like racial bias, it was really an attack on their idea of ANY WOMAN'S com-petence and fitness to occupy that position, and that woman just happened to be Karren. Remember my discussion around the perception of white English managers' competence versus Black managers' competence, white journalists' competence versus Black journalists' competence, heterosexual boxers/footballers/rugby players' competence versus homosexual boxers/footballers/rugby players' competence? None of these biases are personal against any individual member of those discriminated against groups.

I am not so enlightened to feel any differently to most people when it comes to judging the groups mentioned above, though this doesn't apply to Karren Brady, because football is a business and from that perspective, I don't feel women are less competent than men. However, how would I feel about a female football manager of a men's team? I know that, wrongly so, I wouldn't be as accepting in terms of my perception of their abilities. Is it just me? Absolutely not. Don't blame me. This is, once again, what society has told us all about different groups of people and their capabilities.

The story around Gareth Thomas, the former Welsh rugby player, is an interesting one. I know Gareth slightly, both before and after he came out, and because I saw the real macho (in a rugby sense) strong, aggressive and powerful side to him, my perception of him hasn't changed, and I'm sure most people who knew him before and after felt the same way. What would it have been like if he came out while he still played, and more importantly before he started to play? I'm sure if he had, he himself would say he would have faced many more challenges in having a successful rugby career because of the long held, historical behaviours and environment around the sport of rugby, which traditionally has not been particularly inclusive to non-straight men. While we all say we want to see gay sportsmen come out, female football managers, female referees, etc. and we will accept them and judge them in the same way that we do their white male counterparts, the truth is we wouldn't. Understanding and accepting the reasons behind this is the first step in trying to change.

José Mourinho gives a team talk, and it would be easy to accept him ahead of a woman. No offence, please. I'm not judging a woman in this case, but any man giving a team talk, not a famous man but a random man, and a woman giving the exact same team talk. Who would I and the players they are addressing have more faith in? I've had this conversation with many male friends, and a lot of them start off by saying that it wouldn't matter to them; whoever sounded better, their gender wouldn't make a difference. So all the right, politically correct things to say. But after further pressing (and I do that a lot), they finally tell the truth and say the man. They do this after they get comfortable in knowing that I'm not going to judge them negatively by their bias towards the man, because I'm honest enough to tell them I feel the same way. And then we can discuss why we have these biases and unpack the wrongful reasoning in order to try to change our opinions. This is what society needs to fight discrimination – honest, open, non-judgmental dialogue about the reality of discrimination.

Not what we are doing now, which is burying our heads in the sand, passing laws, and attacking certain easy targets to convince ourselves that it isn't prevalent anywhere else.

We all know the reality of the world we live in. I was in Ireland with an ex-teammate of mine doing an event and the host was one of Sky Sports' female presenters. There is a perception that female TV presenters generally have to be attractive and young, rather than focusing on their competence, professionalism and talent. My ex-teammate was talking to this presenter about working at Sky and the fact that all of her fellow female colleagues were 'pretty'. She felt quite insulted by his comments, but he continued by saying that he knows they are talented, but it helps to be pretty too. She became further irritated by these comments the more he repeated them. He felt he was actually paying her two compliments because 'women like to be pretty'. Most men want to be attractive too, it's not a negative or insulting assumption. He was also sincerely complimenting her on her talent, but the more he ended his remarks on the 'pretty' comment, the angrier she became.

I know why she got angry. It's because no matter the reality of her talent, she knows people will assume she got the job primarily for her looks. And deep down, she also knows, no matter how talented she is, that without her looks she probably wouldn't have got the job at Sky because it's a visual industry. So, when confronted with the possibility that something unearned, such as looks, gave you an advantage over another person, you try to convince yourself that it was your ability alone. If you reach into your subconscious mind, you know deep down that there is a widely held perception of a certain 'desirable quality' that you hold, and that has put you above other people with the same ability who are missing this 'desirable quality'.

There are many groups claiming discrimination, but rather than accepting this as a problem which similarly affects other groups in addition to themselves, they simply highlight their own plight and, in many respects, don't see it as a problem for the other groups. For example, on Fox TV in America, there was a heated debate between a white female presenter and a Black man, regarding the treatment of a white school policeman. The policeman had mistreated a Black female student at a school and subsequently lost his job. The female presenter asserted that there was a culture among Black students for disruptive and violent behaviour in school. She went on to say that while the spin on the story would probably be that the student just 'refused to put her mobile phone down', she maintained that the reality was of violent and disruptive behaviour from the Black student. I've seen the video footage from the incident, and if it had been a Black policeman violently overturning a white girl in her chair and dragging her along the floor, there would have been hell to pay, with no sympathy whatsoever for the policeman. That is not the point of the story, however: the point is that as the discussion became more heated, the presenter's true colours came out. The man she was in discussion with challenged her about her assertions about a violent and disruptive culture among Black school children. He cited the numerous instances of white kids going into schools and shooting to death lots of innocent children, without society consequently viewing this as an aspect of white 'culture' in the same way. The conversation descended into a shouting match, culminating with the presenter stating, 'You all have a chip on your shoulder!'

The interesting thing is that these days there is a huge drive in the business community for equality for women in the workplace. Hillary Clinton and other prominent women have spoken out about it, there are committees and steering groups, funding, organisations, etc. And I'm sure this particular Fox TV presenter, given the industry she works in, would have come up against discrimination in the form of sexism at some point in her career; therefore, you would expect her to have empathy with this situation involving another marginalised group. Would she consider herself, or other women who shout from the rooftops about sexism, to have a 'chip on their shoulders'? This is why I say discrimination affects us all, and those in different disenfranchised groups need to be able to come together and empathise with one another.

As an important adjunct to this, Bibaa Henry and Nicole Smallman are two Black women who were horrifically murdered in a London Park, in 2020, less than a year before Sarah Everard was abducted and murdered. We saw the difference not only in the reporting of these murders but the outpouring of horror and empathy towards women by everyone, demonstrating once again not just my point about class and which Black lives matter, but also 'which female lives matter'.

THE BIG BROTHER HOUSE

A few years ago, I was invited to participate in the *Celebrity Big Brother* television programme and when I went to be interviewed, I accepted the offer to participate because of what I thought the agenda would be. It was 2018 and the show's theme was 'Year of The Woman'. Given there was a very diverse cast – including Rachel Johnson (Boris's sister), Ann Widdecombe (ex-Member of Parliament), Maggie Oliver (Greater Manchester Detective Constable), India Willoughby (broadcaster/journalist who is a transgender woman), Courtney Act (a gay drag queen), entertainer Ginuwine and Black reality show star Malika Haqq – I felt it was a chance to have meaningful discussions/debates among a very diverse and disenfranchised group. There were also some young reality celebrities and a very interesting Shane Lynch from the boyband Boyzone. What I was really interested in, was how some of them felt about the discrimination they experienced in their chosen field, or just in their lives generally.

Ann Widdecombe's outlook was interesting. Because of her age, she would likely have experienced more discrimination in the form of sexism throughout her life than everyone else. However, her outlook was that she had to be better than the men to get where she had got to and urged other women to feel the same way. She individualised her experience and had obviously been strong enough to overcome the obstacles in her way. I tried to make the point though, that while this strategy worked fine for her, it might not work for other women who, for whatever reason, might not be as strong as she was. We should not live in a society that requires women to be 'better' than men in order to be considered equal. It seemed the majority of people in that house had a common problem, which was the perception society had of us in relation to the dominant group, regardless of whether we were Black, female, gay, transgender, etc.

While we all argued our points in favour of our own particular group, privately there were disagreements on the grievances of some members of the other groups. This, for me, is the underlying problem with society: we insist on people accepting our gripes about 'our' fight for equality but dismiss other groups' opinions on their own plight. For example, Black heterosexual men might not be concerned with sexism; Black straight men might not be concerned with homophobia.

As an example, I had a discussion with Rachel Johnson (that she may not remember), about a hypothetical time in the future when women are completely equal to men in politics; so imagining that women account for 50 per cent of the Members of Parliament and 50 per cent of the Cabinet. There is a celebration dinner, and as everyone is toasting and drinking champagne, will anyone look around at the group and notice/care/question that there isn't one 'Black' woman among them? After a bit of hesitation, she did say that she would notice this, but I feel fairly certain that, for most people, it wouldn't have been a consideration had it not been brought up.

Once again, the same could be said about any particular group and their considerations for other disenfranchised groups to which they don't belong. The reality is that all of the groups I mentioned suffer from the same problem: the perception that society has about their capabilities, morally, intellectually, etc. in relation to the dominant group, so we should acknowledge and accept each other's grievances.

As I said, the discrimination that all of these groups are subjected to is completely understandable because of the prevailing narrative surrounding them for hundreds of years – women's inability to lead, Black people's inability to think, homosexual's inability to fight in wars, and so on. So rather than just saying that we can't believe that society still sees us that way, we should try to understand 'why' society sees us that way and come up with a solution to the problem. The solution can't be achieved by passing laws to make discrimination illegal, it has to be focused on changing the dominant group's perception of those particular groups. That has to come from an understanding of why we think the way we do about these groups in the first place – a learnt/conditioning/ socialisation/ indoctrination issue.

Much of society used to laugh at Blackface, and now it's unacceptable, but people still laugh at negative caricatures of transgender women, for example. I'm not talking about drag queens on the TV show *RuPaul's Drag Race* where glamourous people dressing as women are depicted, but the pantomime dames we see at Christmas where men portray women in the theatre. The fatter, hairier and uglier these dames are, the more popular/entertaining they seem to be with crowd. This is because that's how we have been historically conditioned to see transgender people. So, for every Caitlyn Jenner or celebrity transgender person who is considered to be attractive and well respected, it does little to change society's opinion of the average transgender person who is still discriminated against.

Getting back to the *Celebrity Big Brother* house – India, who is transgender woman, was also a very interesting personality. She had recently transitioned and was initially full of optimism on entering the house, enthusiastic to show the world who she really was. Her temperament changed though within minutes when Courtney (real name Shane Jenek), the drag artist, entered and India quickly became the most unpopular person in the house due to her negative opinions towards Courtney. I thought this was very unfair because I empathised completely with her. Her experience as a trans person is extremely serious, and her lifelong turmoil and fight would have been equally, or possibly more, difficult than anything experienced by the rest of us in the house. So, when loud and bubbly Courtney came in with a beautiful long skirt that fell off on stage for dramatic effect and people quickly took to her as a figure of fun – not ridicule, but fun – I'm sure India felt that people were then looking at her as the unglamorous/serious caricature.

I could see that when Shane became Courtney and the 'act' started, India became more agitated, and the group had very little sympathy for her which I couldn't understand. Here we were discussing discrimination and being fully convinced about our own feelings of disenfranchisement, yet when one of us showed her discontent, she was accused of being 'too sensitive'. How often have Blacks, women and gay people been told to 'lighten up, nothing is meant by it'. Once again, when 'we're' not being affected, we don't take other groups' problems and opinions seriously.

While being able to fully understand someone else's experience of discrimination is nigh on impossible, you should assume that the conviction you feel about the reality of your own experience is the same conviction that other groups feel about theirs. I've stressed throughout this book that I am not judging anyone, because I unconsciously discriminate like anyone else, but again, it's understandable.

When I was eventually evicted from the house through the backdoor, not by public vote, I was relieved because I missed my wife and kids and was ready to go home. I wasn't aware of what had been shown to the public and was disappointed when I saw a re-run of some of my time on the programme, realising that most of the meaningful discussions I was having weren't shown at all. What was shown however, which was very upsetting, was an edited version of a conversation I had with Courtney that was misinterpreted by some members of the public and resulted in some criticism before I was able to clear it up.

I fully believe that not only are we a product of our environment, but also the period we live in plays a part in our perception of people. So, when Courtney and I had a conversation about why men in general (not me particularly) may feel uncomfortable around gay men, I said that 'they' may get an irrational feeling that if they're in a room alone with a gay man, he may come on to them. I went on to say that men shouldn't feel that way, because if they were in a room with a woman, they wouldn't necessarily feel that 'she' would come on to them, so it really was an irrational feeling. They didn't show the latter part of that conversation, in which I said, tongue in cheek, that being a footballer in the '80s I had no problem being naked with other men and having a feel now and then. It was in jest of course, but I did explain that I was completely comfortable around gay people.

We spoke about other things as well, and I stressed once again that if we are born in a particular period, we think certain things. Even if we rationally know they may not be correct, we can't help thinking them due to our social conditioning. And maybe that will never change. I can't remember what context I used the phrase, 'I was born in a particular time, so can't help thinking the way I do.' By the time I saw the edited conversation when I got out of the house, it sounded something like, 'We feel that if we are in a room with gay men, they are going to come on to us, and being born when I was, I can't help feeling that way.' All words completely taken out of context, order and not my intention at all. The public started criticising me for using my age as an excuse, and after watching the edit, I half understood why they would think that. But as I have spoken about extensively, we have to understand that the media will spin things however they like to get a scandalous story, rather than focusing on what should be an interesting and progressive conversation.

The perception of ourselves is interesting, and although these days we are much more accepting of different groups of people, even the most so-called 'enlightened' of us still aren't immune to our conditioning. I remember reading about a gay marine from the US coming home after a tour, and being greeted by his husband at the dock. They did a re-creation of that famous picture of a sailor from World War II being greeted by his wife in the 1940s, which showed the man lovingly picking up his wife in his arms while she throws her head back in ecstasy at being reunited with her hero. In this modern-day scenario, we had what we would consider to be the more masculine man in his uniform picking up the more feminine man in his arms. My initial shock at seeing the picture, was that the one being caressed lovingly and more dotingly in the arms of his husband, was BLACK . . . and his husband was WHITE. I was surprised at myself for being shocked, because even though we are much more accepting of different groups, and are also more accepting of mixed relationships, both gay and straight, the idea of the more feminine of the couple being the BLACK man caught me by surprise until I consciously rationalised it.

I recently watched a TV programme on sexual harassment from men towards women, where it claimed that there needs to be a political and legal drive to stop this behaviour, and this will lead to a cultural shift in society. But just like racism it has to be the other way around; we have to stop politicising it and make it more of a social and moral crusade. We need to change our cultural/societal patterns and beliefs to eradicate the problem. Rape and sexual harassment have been illegal for many years, but we still see it happening far too often. So just like racism, homophobia and religious intolerance, we have to change PERCEPTIONS before LAWS!

On the television programme *Good Morning Britain,* a clip was played of a commercial in China promoting Royal Milk, which starred Peter Phillips (Princess Anne's son and eldest grandchild of Queen Elizabeth II). I feel strongly that Piers Morgan went on to horribly mock the narrator of the advert, who was speaking in Chinese, with a derogatory impression of the language, saying words sounding like 'ching-chang-chong'. When he was pulled up for this by his co-host, he said he wasn't mocking the language itself, he was only mocking Peter. However, during the advert Peter never actually spoke Chinese, so to my mind Piers' true intentions were clear – he was mocking the Chinese narrator. Following an event like this, you would expect massive criticism from any disenfranchised community who is against racism, but I don't recall anyone in the Black community complaining widely about this – myself not included as I decided to phone the producer twice to make my thoughts clear. Unfortunately, but not surprisingly, the producers took Piers' side.

Why I mention this is because, had Peter been doing an advert in Nigeria and Piers made a derogatory impression of an African narrator, along the lines of saying 'ooga booga', there would have been uproar from the Black community, with thousands of complaints. This story highlights the fact that, as disenfranchised people, we should be calling out this type of behaviour and discrimination against any group, not just our own. And this is the reason that I 'do' conflate the issues.

The high-profile footballers who are so keen to push the narrative around racism in football, who may be looking to become managers in the next five to ten years, should start thinking about inequalities in their industry for Black managers. They are very vocal on social media about the structural bias and racism from Eastern European teams/players yet say nothing about the fact that there are no Black managers in the Premier League (Nuno is Portuguese, and I have already addressed the foreign manager vs British manager dynamic) and only a couple in the three divisions below them. But as I've highlighted throughout the book, people are more concerned about equality only when it affects THEM, so fortunately for current footballers it will be a few more years before this reality becomes theirs. Then maybe the next generation of footballers will go into bat for them rather than trying to get a Romanian fourth official banned (see chapter 11).

THE GOVERNMENT'S VERDICT ON
RACIAL INEQUALITY

Even more insightful is that at the time I am writing this, it's been three days since the Commission on Race and Ethnic Disparities report was released, which has put race relations as well as the fight for equality back decades, and I haven't heard or seen any high-profile footballer speak out against a ruling that is this harmful to the Black community. What little gains that have been made in the last ten years could disappear altogether now that the official governmental verdict is, 'Nothing to see here regarding racial inequalities due to systemic or institutional bias.' However, it did say social media, and individual acts (for example football fans) are a problem; so, footballers will continue to be supported in their fight! Why kick up a fuss then, as once again they personally won't be affected by the ruling. But this should not stop them being concerned, as advocates for the wider Black community, that a report like this is so detrimental with regard to outcomes in schooling, health, incarcerations and job opportunities for those who historically have been, and continue to be, so disenfranchised.

This landmark review states that the UK is not institutionally racist but is in fact a model to the world on diversity! The Sewell Report focuses only on the few Black and female elite people but ignores the fact that millions of Black non elites are left behind and continue to be exploited. Therefore, the status quo isn't threatened too much financially. The commission says that there is NO systemic bias regarding race (gender didn't even make the cut!) and both of these attributes have been relegated below class and geography by their statement that class plays a bigger part in negative outcomes than race. So, from now on, there is no need to invite any more Black people or women to the party because apparently, they already have an equal opportunity to get there and if they don't, it's because they aren't capable of doing so – and not because of any bias. To finish it off, the report recommends scrapping unconscious bias training as it serves no purpose. The truth is the exact opposite of this: it is so necessary for us all to examine our own biases. If we give up on even attempting this then it truly is GAME OVER.

So the elite are posturing that slavery was not just about profit and suffering but was also about giving enslaved Africans the opportunity to TRANSFORM themselves from their inferior culture into a superior 'African-British culture' . . . so that's one benefit of slavery. WOW!!! How do we come back from that? And where do we go from here? Should we start at the beginning trying to convince the next generation that transatlantic slavery was an horrific enterprise? Or go back to the 1700s when that EXACT narrative of giving Africans opportunities to better themselves was sold to the world, and about how slavery is good for the lazy indolent Black man, then wait another 300 years to get to the point we are at now striving for equal opportunities?

The 'firm' or 'establishment' has triumphed wholeheartedly on this one as, once again, they have not only created an illusion of being fair, but they have coerced the RESISTANCE into creating the illusion of all things being as they should be.

Interestingly, after the George Floyd murder case, US President Joe Biden came out and spoke about the now acknowledged systemic racism in America. We sit here in the UK on our high horse saying how terrible race relations are in America, while ignoring our own issues. At least over there they have now taken the step to acknowledge the problem whereas we have regressed and find ourselves pretending there is 'nothing to see here'.

Recently, Prince Harry and his wife, Meghan, have taken the decision to move to America following the racist abuse that Meghan, who is mixed-race, felt she has received from the press in this country. How curious that they have fled to a country that people in England consider to be much more racist than the UK?

Another similar story comparing the different perceptions of racism in the UK vs US involves an interview given by actor Samuel L. Jackson. On a discussion about modern film, he was complaining that English Black actors were coming to America and taking roles of Black historical American figures, such as Martin Luther King, Jr. He was unhappy with this because in his opinion they had not experienced the extent of racism that those in America had; he felt that Black English people were much more accepted by the white community in their own country compared to Black people in America.

People talk about not wanting to conflate separate issues in order to avoid diluting their importance, but I feel that this would be helpful tactic. If we continue to ignore issues that don't personally affect us, we will be going on and on in the same vicious cycle. We have to change our tactics.

9

THE LIES OF HISTORICAL
PERCEPTION

The subject of racism and slavery comes up a lot in pop culture, and many comedians talk about rappers speaking of repatriation to Africa and going back to 'the motherland'. If it wasn't for slavery, where do these millionaire celebrities think they would be in the landscape of African society? Once again, we all believe we have a glorious family past, a young African prince or princess being captured and transported to America as a slave. Well, the reality is that for 99 per cent of us, our forefathers were poor, landless, ordinary members of some tribe which was overpowered, and whose survivors were then sold to the British, Spanish or Portuguese. And for the majority of us whose forefathers had relatives who managed to escape being sold into slavery; if their descendants are still alive (therefore making them relatives of ours) the probability is very high that they, like the majority of people living in West Africa, live under much worse circumstances than we do.

So why do we believe we would be better off if slavery never happened? The transatlantic slave trade was one of, if not the biggest crime against humanity in the history of the world. What my own, and other people's forefathers had to go through was unforgivable. However, once again as I like to do, let's have a sliding doors moment. Let's say we had the chance to go back and change history. Let's use Kanye West as an example (or any millionaire rapper, baller, even the very conscious Chuck D) and say to him – you have a chance to reverse history and stop transatlantic slavery, which means now in 2021, you wouldn't be where you are drinking champagne on Rodeo Drive, driving a Rolls Royce and living in Beverly Hills. You would be in Sierra Leone, Ghana, Liberia or maybe Nigeria, as that's where your forefathers came from. We don't know what you'd be doing or where exactly you would be living or under what circumstances. You could be better off or worse off than you are currently. Would you take that chance? I think we all know the answer to that, and the answer would be the same for the vast majority of the descendants of slaves in the Caribbean and America.

Now, if you ask some Africans if they could go back in time, and have their forefathers captured, sold into slavery and transported to America, meaning that in 2021 they would be living in America doing who knows what, would they take that chance of their lives being better than it currently is? This is not a criticism or judgement of Africa, it's a criticism of the environment and conditions created by colonisation which provided Europe with the wealth derived from the rich natural resources of that continent, with no regard or responsibility to its inhabitants.

When there are horrific, inhumane crimes reported on the news, I can safely say (and maybe it's a generation thing) that a lot of Black people sitting around their TVs have one thing on their mind, and telepathically all together will have one wish: 'Please don't let the perpetrator be a Black man!' The story itself becomes secondary, the specifics of the crimes and atrocities themselves aren't important, just PLEASE DON'T LET HIM BE BLACK. Why do so many of us think that? And hug each other joyously knowing that we can go out into the world tomorrow safe in the knowledge that society won't look at us and think, 'You're all the same.' It's irrational isn't it, or is it? What has this got to do with racial bias? As with most things in this book, it's about perception of ourselves and others, and perception of the way we view ourselves, and the way we view others.

There is an obvious reason why some people feel the way they do towards white society. Most historical facts are grossly exaggerated, whether positively or negatively. There haven't been many people who are as 'bad' or as 'great' as history suggests. The stories have been designed to ensure that certain people will feel superior to others, and others to feel inferior. How would history have treated World War II if Hitler had won? Churchill would have been regarded as a war criminal. If the Moors had conquered Europe, or the Persians beat the Greeks, the historical facts would be slightly different, but the perception of the Moors and Persians would be vastly different.

One important concept that we should all try to understand is that no matter who you are today, Black or white, 99 per cent of us would have gone along with the status quo that existed in any period of time, so don't judge. Don't even judge situations that are occurring in the present.

GENOCIDE IN RWANDA AND BURUNDI

In the '90s I went to Rwanda and Burundi with a charitable organisation to promote peace and reconciliation between the Hutus and the Tutsis. I heard some horrific stories of what happened only a few years earlier during the genocide. I met people involved, who appeared to be just like me – average human beings morally, intellectually and socially. While I was having lunch with one of the men who was looking after us, we were joined by a friend of his for a drink. He appeared to be a normal guy; we laughed, talked about football, life in general, music, food, etc. When the friend left, the guy who was looking after us told me that that gentleman had killed his wife in the genocide. I couldn't believe it because he seemed so normal. He explained that when the killings started, the Hutu army made any Hutu civilians they came across kill Tutsis. Historically Tutsis and Hutus lived peacefully together and would even marry each other. There was no real difference until the Belgians came and 'divided' them (sound familiar?) in terms of perceived worth, with the Tutsis being the 'higher class' and the Hutus the 'working class'. Still though, they interacted peacefully with each other. Because of the Hutu's discontent and what they considered to be discrimination; the genocide started.

The reason why the army forced average Hutu civilians to carry out killings as well, was because they knew that at the end of the war, regardless of the outcome, there would likely be a war crimes tribunal to prosecute the guilty. However, if the whole Hutu population were made to carry out the killings, it would be impossible to prosecute all of them. So, under the threat of not only his life but that of his wife and all of his children, his ultimatum was to kill his wife or watch the army kill her AND his children. So, he did the unthinkable. You might say, 'What a savage, beast, animal . . . how could he?' But I had a drink with him, laughed, spoke about football.

That made me think about what I would have done in his position. I'm John Barnes, middle-class boy from Jamaica, good family, moral and ethically strong: surely, I wouldn't have done what he did? I'd ask the Hutu soldiers to come back tomorrow, then get a club class flight out of there. No, you've got only ten minutes to make up your mind. Okay, I'd offer them Cup Final tickets. No, that wouldn't work. I'd try offering them money. That won't work either. Only five minutes left. I'd say to them, 'Kill me and let my family go.' The moment of truth arrives; my children are lined up with men armed with machetes about to kill them. What do I do? This is not a film, no one is coming to rescue us. Who am I to judge that man?

We frown upon people who commit similar atrocities and crimes and say, 'We would never do that', but how can we judge them? Could John Barnes or any of us under the same conditions, environment and experiences say with any certainty that we would 100 per cent act differently? The ones who say they would, are assuming that they are magically transported into a scenario whereby there is a choice to make, and they very well may make the 'right' choice. But that's not the way to judge what you would really do. It's not John Barnes, born in Jamaica to the family he has; he's the John Barnes born in Kigali (not good or bad) going through whatever he went through in Kigali for his whole life (not right or wrong, good or bad, just his experiences). What decision would he make? I think you would find that the vast majority of people would make the same decisions under identical circumstances. That's why we shouldn't be quick to judge people who do things we say we would never do, but instead be thankful that we live in an environment that doesn't force us to make those kinds of decisions.

Instead of denying our unconscious biases or looking for excuses for the way we really feel about others, let's use that same context, to have a sort of truth and reconciliation as they did in Rwanda. For people to come forward and say, 'Yes, I'm racially biased, but don't judge me too harshly because it's not my fault. It's what I've been taught, learnt, seen, experienced, as have my father and mother and their fathers and mothers before them. It's due to what I see every day in the media which makes me, and people like me, feel the way we do about ourselves and others.'

PERCEPTION VERSUS REALITY

A few years ago, I gave a talk at a college in east London, and met a young Somalian man, about twenty-four years old, who was going to rap on stage before I spoke, about staying in school and being a good person. As we interacted with the students for half an hour before we started, he was the life and soul of the party, making jokes, telling funny stories and being charming. He had everyone, me included, eating out of his hands. When we went on stage, just before he began his rap, he started telling us his story. He had been a child soldier in Somalia. He'd lived in a village that was raided by soldiers; they killed his entire family and most of the people in his village, but he'd managed to escape. He was found by another group of soldiers who gave him an AK-47, drugs and told him to kill other people – which he did. He said he was so small that the AK-47 dragged along the floor behind him. He killed many people until he, and two of his friends, got separated from the group. They walked for miles without food and his friends eventually died of starvation. He said he prayed to God for a bird or another animal to shoot and kill so he could eat, or else he would have to eat his friend's dead body. He said his prayers were answered as he was able to shoot a bird and eat it. He managed to cross the border into Kenya, wandered into a refugee camp and was rescued. At that time, he would have been around twelve years old.

This man purposely engaged with the students before he told them his story; making them like him, making them laugh, making them see how normal he was. This was because he foresaw the perception they would have of him if he just stood up and told them his story, without them seeing that he was just like them. That's an example of how we can have a perception of people that can be vastly different from the reality when we don't know them or their stories.

Martin Luther King, Jr knew that non-violent demonstration was the only way to achieve anything in the civil rights era, because he understood that white society saw Black people as violent and uncontrollable. So, if they reacted in self-defence when they were being brutally beaten at the lunch counters and rallies, white society would have said, 'See how violent and aggressive they are, they need to be kept in check,' Rather than see the truth of the situation, which is, 'They have every right to defend themselves in the face of the treatment that they receive.' So, they had to reason with their attackers, and gain the sympathy of the average white American by being beaten half to death, until those doing and condoning the beatings finally said, 'This isn't right.' Even white civil rights activists didn't necessarily believe in moral and intellectual equality, they just knew that society was wrong for treating other human beings (even if they're 'inferior') in the way they did.

If we want to strive for equality, it is extremely important to expose the lies that have historically been told about disenfranchised and marginalised groups. Those lies have been more influential in creating the perceptions of how we see ourselves and others than the actual truth. The lies have been around for such a long time and have been allowed to fester, condition, inform our thinking and be absorbed by society to become the natural order of things.

After the American Civil War, during the Reconstruction Era Black people were given voting rights and property rights without the actual perception of their worth and equality being considered. Years later, the 'Jim Crow' laws came into being which not only suppressed voting rights, but enforced educational, vocational and social laws for segregation that negatively impacted Black people. This continued into the late '60s, so many years after they had initially attempted to pass laws to make life more equal for Black people. And how much has changed for the masses up until now? This is the reason why I say laws alone can't truly change things, as was demonstrated back then. The only way for meaningful change is to change PERCEPTIONS before laws.

Hundreds and thousands of years ago, before the ideas of race or racial hierarchy as we know it existed, different groups (races) of people encountered each other and their mutual respect and perception of each other wasn't based on our modern ideals of worthiness, it was based on power, wealth and elitism. So, the whitest people on earth could encounter the Blackest people, with the flattest noses and biggest lips, but if these Black people were the dominant group in that area, they would command the utmost respect from those white people. There was no question of them being inferior because they were Black. Once colonialism prevailed, the idea of racial hierarchy based on the inferiority of Blackness came about and this led to all of the racial problems we faced today.

THE HISTORY OF SLAVERY

Transatlantic slavery originally had nothing to do with racism, it was economics. This idea of a Black identity didn't exist. In the West, we as Black people may identify with each other because, due to transatlantic slavery, we were all just Black. In the early days of slavery, it was more likely that there was a sense of identity with one's tribe and culture as opposed to a sense of racial identity. In some cases, you were chained to your enemies who you hated, had been at war with and never even felt racially connected to. But by the time the next generation came along, a Black identity rather than a tribal identity took over.

While people in America and England condemn 'Black on Black' crime and call for us all to come together because we are the same race; this was not the case back then in Africa, and in some areas still isn't the way a lot of Africans view the situation. So, it was never a case of selling your brother or people of your own tribe. Slavery was never about race or racism; it was about greed and commercialism. Some of my Black friends who are aware of this also say, yes, we understand that, but the type of slavery that Africans practised among themselves was one whereby they would intermarry and become part of the family eventually. They didn't know how harsh the conditions of the Middle Passage were or the fate that lay ahead for the slaves going across to the New World.

That may be true, although the instances of slaves integrating into other tribes were few and far between. It would also be after many years of servitude and not forgetting that their family, and other members of their own tribe, had likely been butchered, hunted, chained up and treated as slaves. African slavery certainly wasn't a walk in the park or a nice experience. Secondly, do you think for one minute that if the African chiefs did know everything about what the slaves who were sold would have to go through, they would have said, 'Sorry, we won't sell them to you, because you will treat them too badly'?

So, while we see 'Black on Black' violence that may occur in some West African countries and describe it as 'Black people killing themselves', they don't see it that way. It shouldn't be posed that way in order to denigrate Black people; for hundreds of years, white people killed each other in European wars without it being labelled 'white on white' crime.

The point of the above is to explain how the perspective of Black people towards white people has been affected by their perception of the situation they find themselves in now, and the sole culprit behind it. Maybe, if we as Black people understood the reality behind African slavery, while still knowing that there is inequality, this may temper our feelings towards white people. Once again, I have to keep stressing that this isn't a criticism of Africa, Africans or their part in the slave trade, it's just a reality that could help our perception of the situation.

IDENTITY AND INEQUALITY

Before we treat someone as equal, we have to see them as equal. Before we treat someone with respect, we have to see them as worthy of our respect and not the other way around.

I have many Israeli and Palestinian friends, and the Israeli—Palestinian conflict is probably the most complex problem in the world today. Here are two of issues to consider: worthiness and support. As far as worthiness is concerned, I've often thought about who is more worthy of our empathy, and how do they view themselves as well as each other.

Consider when the time comes every now and then for a prisoner exchange between Israel and the Palestinians, and there is an Israeli soldier who isn't a high ranking officer or someone from the Israeli elite, just an ordinary soldier who has been kidnapped by the Palestinians, and they demand the release of some Palestinian prisoners, they say they want 100 in exchange for one Israeli, and the Israelis sometimes comply. What does that do to the psyche of the Israelis? Does it make them feel that one of them is worth 100 Palestinians? Conversely, how does it also make the Palestinians feel, because although they may be getting 100 of their comrades back, if Israel offered them 25 prisoners, they would reject the proposal . . . as it seems that even they themselves regard one Israeli to be worth more than 25 Palestinians? Would asking for a one-to-one exchange empower them more/less and change the perception of their respective individuals' worth?

The other issue of support for either group, which is more complicated as former Labour leader Jeremy Corbyn found out, is: can you support the Palestinian cause and not be anti-Semitic? Not according to some Jewish people, because some feel you can't separate the state from the religion. This causes huge problems regarding the idea of race, religion and ethnicity, and is not as cut and dried as we make it out to be.

Shamima Begum, a British-born woman who left the UK aged fifteen to support the Islamic State group in Syria, has been accused of very serious charges relating to terrorism, the details of which have been widely discussed, and there is no question that she has a legal case to answer. Fortunately, we have a very robust, although imperfect, legal system which is well equipped to deal with these types of cases of which there have been many. The Home Office successfully argued that their interpretation of Bangladeshi law gave Shamima Begum Bangladeshi citizenship by descent and subsequently revoked her British citizenship. This was not uncontroversial and was disputed by opposing experts in Bangladeshi law and by the Bangladeshi government themselves and is currently under appeal.

For me, the more worrying story here is about the precedent being set for a multi-tier British citizenship and the message the government are sending regarding the level of respect they afford to different nations around the world. This is why I think that she should not only be allowed entry to the UK to complete her appeal but that her citizenship should be reinstated, and her case should be heard like any other British citizen should expect.

Let's not get into the nitty gritty of Bangladeshi citizenship law and ignore the extreme arrogance of assuming that the British interpretation of that law is more accurate than that of the Bangladeshi government. Let's give the Home Office the benefit of the doubt. The wider implications of stripping even a genuine dual citizen of their British citizenship appear not to have been considered.

If Shamima Begum were a dual citizen, what message does that send to other dual citizens? As in immigrant to this country and having called it home for forty-four years, should I be worried that if my British-born children committed a horrendous crime then the Home Office would consider seeking the revocation of their citizenship? They may or may not be successful depending on the laws of the country of descent, in this case Jamaica, but would this approach be even considered? It seems that it would be, and the message is – you're only British as long as we say you are. This is not true of 'white British' citizens, and this is a problem.

Finally, this case highlights the inherent bias that we demonstrate in our approach to dealing with different nations. Imagine if Shamima Begum were a citizen of France/Germany/ USA. Would we expect them to deal with a British born and raised accused terrorist because they were entitled to/held dual citizenship? Or would we take responsibility for our own problems and respect the fact that they would not be interested in taking on our problem citizens that we no longer want?

My concern is that the take home message from this story is that 'white British' citizens are British come what may and citizens with heritage based in Western countries that we respect are possibly safe too, while everyone else's status as British is subject to conditions. I don't believe that this reflects the 'British values' that have been so proudly invoked in recent public discourse and risks setting a legal precedent for a multitier citizenship system.

WHITE SUPREMACY

The starting point of understanding racial hierarchy is white Western superiority. Not all white people will be considered superior – women, working class, northern, Eastern European and a myriad of other examples – but that is NOT because of their whiteness. Some Black people will be considered as equal: footballers (good ones), actors, singers, TV presenters, scientists, etc. but the group they belong to isn't considered equal. They have been 'elevated' out of that group. So, the solution is to change the way we feel about those white people who aren't seen as superior and to change the way we feel about the Black race as a whole, not just to only accept elite Black people. The nuances of discrimination as far as class, race, gender, religion and sexuality are concerned are quite complex, but if we want to deal with race specifically then that's the starting point in my opinion. And once again, we as Black people have to stop wanting to be elevated out of Blackness, but instead should strive to change the PERCEPTION of Blackness as a whole.

Why do Black people shout the loudest about racial discrimination? In my opinion it's because we are the most discriminated against group left of the 'original' races of mankind. We aren't necessarily the most discriminated group in history; you only need to look at indigenous peoples in both North and South America, or aboriginal Australians and the horrors they faced. But because their races/cultures have nowadays either become absorbed or exterminated from mainstream society, their existence and rights have been so marginalised it's almost as though the fight doesn't count anymore. Give Native Americans, casinos and tax breaks in an effort to 'appease' everybody and you can forget about all of the wrong which was done to them less than 200 years ago. So, when I say that Black people are the most disenfranchised group 'left over', that's because Africans were colonised, and continue to be economically colonised, so our destiny isn't at this moment in time in our own hands. The other racially disparate groups were able to become masters of their own destiny. While the ideology concerning their worthiness puts them below white people, but above Black people, it doesn't actually impact on their independence or financial strength at this time.

WHITE PRIVILEGE

It is a fact that all white people benefit from white privilege. Yes, a lot of white people suffer from a lack of privilege in terms of class, finances or geographical location, but not because of their skin colour. So, when actor Laurence Fox denies his white privilege by saying that lots of working-class white kids are discriminated against, he is ignoring the fact that the discrimination they face is not to do with the fact they are white, it's to do with class. And secondly, he can't deny or argue against his own white privilege just because some inner-city white boys may not be privileged. What does that have to do with him? Many women, Muslims and Black people are also privileged (myself included), but in these cases our gender, religion or colour aren't the reason for our privilege. Whereas the only group of people who are afforded a privilege for the sole reason of belonging to that group, is white people.

I was watching a *HARDTalk* programme, that was grilling a right-wing French intellectual about the racial problems in France, and he was saying it was a problem with Muslims. When he was accused of inciting Islamophobia, he replied that it wasn't Islamophobia, but it might be racism! When confronted by another intellectual, he said that this person wasn't an expert, because he was talking about Muslims that don't speak Arabic, but the Arabic speaking Muslims were the problem. So, if what he says is right, and it's an Arabic speaking Muslim problem, then it's not racism, as Muslims of different races speak Arabic. Confusing? If so-called intellectuals can't make sense of what is or is not racism, what chance have we lay people got? The intellectual went on to say, 'France gives them an opportunity to renounce their religion and become just "French."' However, you can have French Christians and Jewish people don't have to renounce their religion to be French. So why can't Muslims stay Muslim and also be French?

White privilege is very real and is a determining factor, on a basic level, in simplistically explaining the differences between the Black and white experience. However, if we as Black people want 'allies' (mainly white people) to empathise with our predicament, we have to use different examples to make the point. We continue to use the experiences of elite, privileged Black people to highlight the fact that despite their 'elite-ness', they suffer from bias on a level that the white working-class don't. This shows that the negative perception of Blackness at times supersedes the class and elite aspect of real life. However, this then creates a bigger problem. White privilege resonates, and is more tangible among Black people, than it is among the white working-class. This is because no matter the reality of white privilege, the average white working-class person who may not have a job, housing or education, who struggles daily to feed their family, and has been convinced to feel that their misfortunes are due to the benefits given to 'others' instead, understandably doesn't feel the BENEFIT OF THEIR WHITE PRIVILEGE. If we keep showing privileged Black superstars who ever so often experience an absence of privilege due to their race, while for the majority of the time experience what the white working-class can only dream of, it turns the white working class against the Black struggle.

In July 2021, the England football team made the final of the European Championships. After an exciting tournament with huge support from fans across the country the final was unfortunately lost on penalties. Three Black England players – Marcus Rashford, Jadon Sancho and Bukayo Saka received horrendous racial abuse after missing their penalties.

This, along with the many other examples I have used in the book, is a classic case of 'when you win you're a hero, but when you lose, you're Black', as we have seen time and time again.

There was sympathy from a lot of right-minded people for the abuse on social media that they received, and many pleas for support for them from a mental health and basic respect perspective. A few days after the events, videos were posted of a couple of the players on a private plane with champagne on the way to a holiday in Ibiza. Now, these Black players absolutely have every right to live their lives in whichever way they choose regardless of our perception of them, and to enjoy what they have earnt as any other young successful person would do. However unfortunately, this image of 'living the highlife', is bound to make it difficult for a struggling white working-class person to feel empathy/sympathy towards the plight of the poor discriminated against Black man and this is a huge problem we face in our society. As I said, they have every right to do as they please with their hard-earned cash, but if we as a group want 'allies' and people to understand our plight, then unfortunately we have to be more aware of how that may look to the very people we are trying to get onside.

That's why, as I've always said, we should instead use stories of the plight of the Black working class as examples of racial bias in the hopes that white working-class people can empathise more. We should explain that Black working-class people experience all the negative aspects of life that their white counterparts do, as well as the ADDED negative perception of Blackness. Only through doing this can we move forward in a more enlightened fashion.

PART THREE

'I look to a day when people will not be judged by the colour of their skin, but by the content of their character.'

Martin Luther King, Jr

10

PROPAGANDA: WHO ARE THE HEROES AND VILLAINS?

'Until lions have their own historians, tales of hunting will always glorify the hunter.'

Chinua Achebe, Nigerian novelist

How is the perception of racial superiority subtly perpetuated? By the media, for one. Not every conflict between different groups is a race or hate crime, or racially motivated. We used to be able to have a fight, or argument with white people without it being racial. But we've now gone beyond that to label most, if not every, unpleasant confrontation between different races of people as a racial incident. Why can't it just be a disagreement between two people who happen to be of different races? This isn't a Donald Trump fake media line, it's an observation of the way the media in the West reports on issues in the world relating to ourselves and others both at home and abroad.

We are used to hearing about 'Jamaican Yardie drug rings' in London, 'Nigerian money scams', 'Muslims grooming young girls': all of this creates a negative impression in our minds, not only of the drug dealing, money-laundering or grooming part of the story, but of the Jamaican, Nigerian and Muslim side of it. You'll never read 'white' or 'English' paedophile ring exposed, or 'white' or 'English' gang kill their rivals. And while this may seem trivial and inconsequential, to quote my old football coach at Liverpool, Ronnie Moran, 'The little things make the big things.' Because if you keep repeating the same catchphrases they will eventually stick in the minds of the general public.

Because of our passive acceptance that we are all equal, although that has been eroded by history, we will never condone any conscious expression of racial superiority. So, statements such as 'whites are better than Blacks', 'all Muslims are terrorists', 'Jewish people are greedy' aren't headlines we will accept or agree with. However, when there are headlines like the ones I mentioned earlier (and we do see hundreds of stories printed like this), the negative perceptions about the groups mentioned sink into our subconscious and we form an adverse opinion of them.

Going through the newspapers every day, we subliminally see discriminatory reporting which chips away at our feeling of non-bias. There is a story of an altercation on the train in Germany when a German OAP is attacked by a man of 'Eastern European' or 'Arab' appearance; this went viral at a time when Angela Merkel was beginning to adopt an open-door immigration policy. The assailant could well be German, but his obvious physical difference gives the media an opportunity to make a political point.

There is another story of a white man in Charleston, South Carolina, who killed nine Black churchgoers, and describes him as being 'self-radicalised'. Had he been Muslim, he would have been described as a 'radicalised' Muslim, which implies that the Islamic religion has something to do with radicalisation. There is also a story in the *Daily Mail* newspaper headlined, 'Woman Rapist Led Gang of Paedophiles for a Decade.' Can you guess what colour they are? I'll give you a clue: had they been Black or Muslim, the headline would have read something like, 'African woman', 'gang of Nigerian paedophiles', 'burkha-wearing woman', 'gang of Muslim men', etc. This once again chips away at our perception of 'all those people'.

But if the perpetrator happened to be white, his or her wrongdoings would be seen to have nothing to do with their 'whiteness'.

From a Black perspective, because of our history and the perception of our worth based on it, we as Black people talk about being Black and proud. This is an interesting concept; we don't hear of people being proud to be white. It makes the need to feel 'Black pride', or to celebrate Black history month or other occasions devoted to Blackness seem strange. There are calls to create awards for Black player of the year, Black Oscars, etc. Whereas all mainstream awards aren't labelled white, they are open to everyone, but because there is a disproportionate group of people who are the beneficiaries, some people feel the need to create another category based on race. This would be viewed as an inferior category and while I'm not a fan of it, maybe it's necessary to reward those involved for their efforts and talent.

THE SHOW MUST GO ON

What about the role the media plays in underpinning our perception of ourselves and others? If you go back to the early days of Hollywood, when experiences of adventure, exploration and conquest were at the forefront of everyone's aspirations, the conquest of the Indians and Africans by the honourable white men who wanted to 'help them' was the predominant narrative. So, all the cowboy films of the '50s and '60s were about the evil and savage 'Red Indians' massacring innocent women and children, then the sight of our white heroes fighting for what's right would make us cheer. Personally, I always wanted to be a cowboy because Indians were 'bad', so we were taught.

Tarzan was an even more interesting phenomenon. Here is a white baby adopted by apes (I'm sure there could have been Black babies to adopt, who grew up in the jungles of Africa to become king of the apes). In *Def Comedy Jam* there is a hilarious routine of a comedian talking about this. He describes how Tarzan can speak to all the animals, knows how to avoid danger and is the strongest; while Black people who had lived there for hundreds of years kept falling in the quicksand, were feeble and 'couldn't say boo to a motherfucking monkey'.

Now, you could argue that these were only films, mere entertainment, but now the empowerment of one group and examples of their dominance were there for everyone, including impressionable children, to see.

How many war films have we watched showing the good guys overcoming the bad guys? In the old war films, it would be the fight against the Germans in which a few English or American heroes killed lots of Germans. Then there were Vietnam War films, depicting Americans killing even more incompetent Vietnamese. It's taken on a new direction now. Most of the war films are either against African warlords or Muslim terrorists. It's made clear the superiority and ease with which our heroes dismantle those foolish, incompetent Africans who outnumber our heroes hundreds to one but can't shoot straight and are so cowardly that it's laughable. It's only a film though . . .

How sad do we feel when just one or two of our heroes die, because we absolutely empathise with them. He's just like us, he has a wife and two kids, he lives in a little town just like ours. The two hundred people he killed aren't like us, they're animals who just kill innocent babies. They deserve to die. That's what we would have thought of our Somali rapping child soldier who performed at the college in east London, had we not met him in person beforehand.

Remember another of our heroes, Gordon of Khartoum. One of Britain's greatest generals, or so we are told. The old film shows him being the last one alive as the Muslim Dervishes swarm across the complex, killing all the British soldiers.

He waits upstairs in the barracks as masses of the enemy swarm in shouting like savages, waving their swords and spears at the bottom of the stairs while he majestically and regally appears at the top. They stand in silence, scared, staring wide-eyed at a man so much greater than themselves. He walks down the stairs, does up his tie, holds his head high and stares at them as they cower and bend their heads in fear of him. As he glides through the crowd, one 'coward' in the back throws a spear and pierces his heart, killing him. Once the great man is dead, the enemy start shouting and dancing over his body. Seeing this, who do we respect more? And is that the reality?

While modern films seek to try to convince us that the West is a place of equality for all and try to tick boxes, they hide the reality of what our society is really like. By criticising other societies, they fool even themselves that all is well within their environment.

The Dam Busters. What a film! An army officer, with his posh voice speaking like he'd recently had elocution lessons, calls out to his Black dog, 'Nigger! Nigger! Where are you boy? Has anyone seen Nigger?' I'm sure when the film was released in theatres in the '50s no one batted an eyelid. Even those watching it in the '70s and '80s would not likely be shocked or criticise this; and those people, are the same people who around now. I have no issue with these films. We created a society and environment in which they were accepted.

REWRITING HISTORY

Think about all the historical stories of greatness, compassion, bravery and righteousness in the face of a cowardly and vicious enemy. In reality, did our heroes actually act in a similar fashion in the conflicts they were involved in?

Britain in the last 400 years has probably been involved in more conflicts and conquests than any other country in the world, and I can't remember too many tales of barbarism, torture, raping and pillaging, or any forms of dishonourable behaviour from our heroes. Considering we were told that the enemy regularly did those things, our boys must have to be morally and ethically superior not to react in the same way. We're told that we managed to rule the world by people gladly accepting us as their masters because we were fair and honourable in our treatment of them. We saved them from their despotic leaders, or other European nations who wouldn't have been as kind to them. Well, tell that to the Boer civilian women and children of South Africa who were detained in concentration camps during the Boer War. Or to the Mau Maus of Kenya who were systematically hunted down and slaughtered by the British. Or to the victims of the Amritsar massacre, in the early twentieth century, where hundreds of peaceful protesters and religious pilgrims in India were fired upon and killed by British soldiers. Wait, that all can't be true, we would never do that! That's what 'other people do'!

So, what is the point of these stories we are told? They are used to show how the perception of 'our' British superiority over other people came about and continues to be ratified.

I remember seeing not so long ago on the news that the UK's 4G network coverage was not in the Top 25 worldwide. What?! We are Britain and there are some of the most 'backward' countries ahead of us? We are below Romania, Bulgaria, Morocco, Colombia? Impossible! We're Britain, these countries look up to us and need us more than we need them.

What are historical facts? If we were to go back in time, we would see the events of history in very much the way they actually happened. But if we read books about history today, which depict an interpretation of the facts, our perception would differ somewhat from the reality. For example, history books say, 'Livingstone discovered Victoria Falls'. No, he didn't. Black people had been living near there and knew about them and had been to them hundreds of years before he was even born, and then some of those people lead him there. Okay, so he was the first European to see them. So what? Why does that make him great? Now if he'd actually discovered them, that would have made him great. Oh yeah, I forgot, history said he discovered them. Okay, he is great.

Let's take our greatest Western hero, Jesus Christ. The reality is that Jesus Christ would have looked more like Osama Bin Laden than Robert Powell or Brad Pitt. But what are the images we traditionally see of Jesus? They have darkened him up a bit more in recent times, but nevertheless he and his followers still look a bit more like Clive Owen than Saddam Hussein (although their enemies coincidentally all look like Colonel Gaddafi). 'It's only a film, it's only a film,' people say. But would the same film be successful if you reverse the roles of the people involved? No. Why not? Because in the West we want to associate all that's good, moral, right, with people that look like 'us', i.e. white people, never mind the 'facts', 'reality' or 'truth' of history. In order to justify our feeling of superiority, we have to be seen as the ones who have made the world what it is today.

If you knew more about Eastern civilisations prior to the 1500s, which gave Europeans the knowledge to not only conquer the world but to make advancements in science, medicine and education, you would think differently about moral and intellectual equality. I keep coming back to the idea of race and identity, and I love using history and film as an indicator of our perceptions. Take a film that, like many other young boys, I loved: *10,000 BC*. The original, with Raquel Welch . . . what a film! Raquel and other beautiful cave women in loin-cloth dresses with full hair and make-up. Yes, it was like that back in those days, running away from sabre tooth tigers and fighting other tribes, until the asteroid hit the earth and left them to rule the world together. *10,000 BC* is the way the world should be: the two warring tribes were comprised of a white, blonde-haired, blue-eyed civilised tribe (Raquel's lot), and a white, dark-haired, brown-eyed tribe. The blonde-haired tribe spoke an intelligible language, were kinder, gentler, smarter. You may have thought they would lose the fight against the stronger, more brutal darker people, but their intelligence made them superior.

The filmmaker couldn't have made the dark-haired, brown-eyed people superior because the movie-goers wouldn't have agreed with blonde-haired, blue-eyed people being inferior, even though everyone was white. So even among all white people, there was, and still is a perception of superiority residing in the quintessential white person as personified by blonde hair and blue eyes. Why is that? Because, until recently not 'all' white people were considered 'white'. Not so long ago, Italians, Spaniards, Eastern Europeans (the ones from the Caucasus region anyway), most of whom had darker, olive-coloured skin, were not considered white. I don't know how the Irish got lumped in with those other groups. So, when they became accepted as white, there still had to be, as there is in all cultures, a hierarchy among the white race (remember light-skinned Black people in the Caribbean, the caste system in India, the social distinctions between Hutus and Tutsis). So even among our Western heroes, there is a type of hero that we like to identify with. Sometimes he doesn't actually even have to be like us. But he is the one whom we aspire to be like. The fact that he tends to be blonde-haired and blue-eyed once again places in our subconscious the idea that this is what honour, intelligence and integrity looks like. So never mind that I see him killing hundreds of people who look like me. I want him to win because I want to be like him.

INDIVIDUALISING HUMANITY

It is interesting when we think about the American mantra in war, 'no man left behind'. Twenty men will not only risk their lives but sacrifice themselves to save just one of their comrades, because of the idea that one of their soldiers is worth a hundred of 'us'. The difference is that we will individualise that one person and the terrible experience he or she is going through. Therefore, our feeling of empathy towards 100 specific individuals belonging to one group, is much more powerful than our feeling of empathy towards one group of 100 individuals who we don't really 'see' as people like us. So, when we see hundreds of refugees from Syria or Iraq, or thousands of starving malnourished kids in Somalia, we see them as one group of unfortunate people. If we were to individualise them, we would feel more sympathy/empathy for them.

When you hear stories of people who adopt children, even Black kids from orphanages in Africa, they will say frequently that when they walked among the hundreds of kids in the orphanage, there was 'something' about the one they chose. They 'individualised' that child and saw their 'humanity', which separated them from the rest. And that's how we should see each 'individual' refugee or displaced starving person.

If you take the film *The Expendables* as an example, with terrorists in an African country fighting against the 'good guys', there are scenes of the 'bad guys' being killed in their hundreds. The killings appear to occur in milliseconds, so we don't identify with them because it all happens so quickly.

We dehumanise them, as opposed to the deaths of our heroes in which we see the pain, humanity and the emotional element of life that you presume one would have as they cling on until their dying breath. So, therefore we have more empathetic feelings towards them. Once again, this has nothing to do with racism, rather it has to do with us feeling sympathy or empathy towards a particular person, or groups of people, and the group who we have come to empathise with, are the 'stars' of the show. And just like the 'stars' of life, they generally happen to be white. I say generally white, because if one of the 'stars' is Denzel Washington, we absolutely empathise with him because he gets to die with honour, and in such a way that we see him as just like 'us'. So, if he kills twenty white men, we are still on his side, because he represents what's good.

I say it doesn't necessarily have anything to do with racism, because if over the last few hundred years we had been exposed instead to images, pictures and films of blonde-haired, blue-eyed people being treated in an inhumane fashion and dying seemingly without feeling, we as a society would view them in the exact same way that we view Black people today. So, it's not personal, it's about whichever the disenfranchised group happens to be. That always has to be someone and unfortunately for Black people, women and the LGBTQ community, it's those groups. Once we understand and accept our culture-based biases in society and ourselves, we can do something about changing them.

As much as we should be evolving into a more compassionate and inclusive society, with Donald Trump winning the US presidential election in 2016 and the UK's Brexit decision, I'm not so sure that this is occurring. I'm not criticising the voters who supported these outcomes, but I am questioning their motives for the way they voted. In my opinion, both Donald Trump's and the pro-Brexit campaigns were run on an 'us versus them' philosophy, in which people were convinced that the main reason for their lack of opportunities was because of 'foreigners' – not the foreigners we identify with, but the Muslims, the Eastern Europeans and the Syrian refugees, etc.

This has happened throughout history – the socio-economic 'elite' convincing the rest of society that the decisions they make are for the good of the people. This is done by finding an imagined enemy and simply feathering their own nests rather than actually acting for the good of the people. It was a fairly simple thing to do in ancient times, because people back then didn't know anything about the so-called enemy in faraway lands, and just accepted what they were told about them. Today they have to be much more sophisticated in their propaganda, because in modern times we live among the so-called enemy in our communities, and we know that they are no different to us. So, it's very helpful to the cause when a Muslim, Communist, or African despot commits a horrific crime as this can be used to convince Western society that this is what all Muslims, Communists and Africans are really like, and they have to be dealt with appropriately.

WHAT CAN WE LEARN FROM HISTORY?

In my opinion, the main reason for analysing or judging events of the past, is the effect it has on the present and possibly the future. The debate over the majority of incidents in the past regarding who is right or wrong, good or bad, innocent or guilty, accountable or not, differs from group to group. However, if those incidents are major factors in societies' ills today, they should be examined. We spend so much time and energy attacking or defending past heroes/villains that we can't see the wood for the trees and focus on things we had no control over and can't change. But we can change the present and future by understanding the past, and the reasons behind the events of yesteryear.

A typical example would be King Leopold of Belgium who was one of the most evil men in the world in his treatment of the people of the Congo and his murder and exploitation of them. On the contrary, his loyalty and benevolence towards Belgium, in gifting the vast majority of his fortune to the state to make it the country it is today, made most Belgians view him as a hero. So, of the vast majority of white Belgians who have benefited from the colonisation of the Congo and see him as a hero, versus the minority Congolese immigrants in Belgium whose forefathers suffered at the hands of his colonisers and see him as evil – who is right? This debate rages on many levels all over the Western world regarding heroes and villains. So, as I mentioned at the beginning, we should be more concerned with the effect those historical events have on present-day discourse and perceptions rather than the rights or wrongs of the past, although this should obviously still be acknowledged and discussed.

In the argument against using historical events such as slavery to explain outcomes for Black people today, some say we could look at other historical events whereby white people were also 'colonised and exploited' but nowadays don't use this as an excuse for their present conditions. For example, when Britain was under Roman rule, the people were equally as exploited and disenfranchised as Black slaves were during the slave trade; however white people today do not call on this time and use it as an excuse for any struggles they face today. But why that argument is invalid is because there is no present Roman Empire that continues to negatively affect white English people and stunt their opportunities and growth. This same idea could be applied to the Muslims who conquered Spain or the Mongolian Empire which reached the gates of Vienna. These leading empires are no longer powerful or threatening, so it is meaningless to compare the dynamics.

This is how the propaganda machine works: to get the nationalists onside you have to convince them that the reason for their discontent is someone else and not the failings of the institutions that are supposed to be providing for them. So, you look for the easiest and weakest target with no way of defending themselves, you exaggerate their power and sit back and watch the fight unfold. The best way to get the Black, disenfranchised community onside is to do the same thing. But even better, get some Black allies on your side to endorse it, make it appear even more legitimate. Now pick individuals to criticise: the Romanian fourth official's alleged use of racist language towards a coach in a Champions League match (see chapter 11), the thirteen-year-old Burnley fan for purported racial abuse of a

Spurs player, Bulgarian fans, Liam Neeson, Peter Beardsley, Amy Cooper and any other weak scapegoat we can find. Then promote a Black elite person into the organisation, make them the authority and voice to be listened to (as long as they are criticising the 'right people') and if another Black person doesn't support that narrative, get other Black people to criticise and try to turn the masses against them. Sit back and let them battle it out and see who influences their people more. The winner will always be the one with the bigger and better platform, no matter what the truth is. How do you think the current narrative surrounding Black people started? By convincing the white mainstream community that Black people were inferior, unintelligent and needed to be educated by a superior group. We now have Black people saying the same thing to other groups because we have been tricked or coerced or recruited to do the establishment's work for them, despite the fact we ourselves were historically adversely affected the most by this very tactic.

In 2020, Sainsbury's produced a Christmas advert featuring a Black family celebrating together in their home. It caused a huge stir among the British population with thousands of complaints and threats to boycott the company as some people said they 'couldn't relate to this picture of Christmas'. Rewind to the previous year when there had been a Christmas advert produced by Aldi depicting a family of cartoon carrots! No complaints about being able to relate there?! For years, no one batted an eyelid if there wasn't a Black or ethnic minority representation in adverts then the few times there is, there is uproar.

THE SUPERIORITY/INFERIORITY COMPLEX

Our British sense of superiority is actually only based on events that happened historically up until sixty years ago. Since then, we have actually been just like most other nations in our 'greatness' or 'average-ness'. Everything we achieved from the 1600s up until the end of colonisation was based on theft and exploitation, which at the time the whole of Europe were also trying to do to the rest of the world, just not as adeptly as Britain. Our actions were sold as altruism and being moral and intellectually beneficial to the wider world. Paradoxically, since the 1960s, when the world changed and other countries 'caught us up', there was, and still remains, some sense of British inferiority compared to other nations, e.g. foreign football managers being superior, Europeans speaking multiple languages, but we still remember the 'glory years' and often struggle balancing both narratives and deciding which one is real.

The idea of multilingualism being a marker of intelligence is interesting in this superiority/inferiority conundrum. If a Belgian person speaks French, German, English, Flemish and Dutch they are considered intelligent. If a West African speaks English, French and three more African dialects, that isn't seen as a marker of intelligence as 'his' languages aren't necessarily considered as those worthy enough of respect.

In the race context, there was no concept of the 'white' race before the necessity to justify the enslavement of Africans. Creating an 'inferior' race simultaneously facilitated the belief in and the creation of a 'superior' race.

Before the theory of all humans evolving from the same modern human race who wandered out from Africa to populate the four corners of the world, the West had a very different opinion. They held the idea of racial superiority based on the theory that other groups were inferior because they had mixed with other archaic and savage humanoids. They believed the 'pure homo sapien' was European. Neanderthals and other ancient humans were considered backward and responsible for the inferiority of the other races. It has now been proven that some Europeans have a small amount of Neanderthal DNA and there was in fact mixing between homo sapiens and Neanderthals for most of the world's ancestors. Well, 200 years ago that idea was used to prove the inferiority of other races, but now that it's the Europeans who have DNA from a 'backward' human, the narrative among some is that that's the reason why Europeans are SUPERIOR and actually Neanderthals weren't as stupid as we thought, we should focus on their strength! The strongest, most dominant community will always control the narrative regardless of contradictions.

'YOU'RE ALRIGHT, IT'S JUST THE OTHERS . . .'

I have a theory that immigration before colonisation would have been much better, because society would have 'taken people as they found them' without having negative precon-ceived perceptions about groups of people told to them via propaganda stories before they ever even came into contact with them. Unfortunately, because colonisation came first, this negative propaganda was fed to people to indoctrinate their opinion on people from faraway lands. But when they finally met a person from that group, who turned out to be 'just like them', society convinced itself that it wasn't racially biased because they got on with any given individual of a different race. That's where the 'well, you're alright, it's just the others' narrative came from and that's who I call the 90 per centers. Because colonisation and tales of racial (national) superiority came first, by the time society came into contact with different groups of people, it already held so many negative perceptions. And that works both ways, with positive perception, when reverse immigration took place and Europeans went to the colonies.

Throughout history the most powerful weapon has been the human mind and the propaganda and influence we can exert over others. Forget guns and bombs, no matter what physical weapons we have, if we can convince people through our influence, they will do our bidding. So, convincing people of racial superiority and inferiority has been the most influential dynamic in racism.

Commentator Piers Morgan added fuel to the flames on *Good Morning Britain* when he decided to highlight a ridiculous debate concerning chess being racist because the rules of the game say the white piece moves first. In discussing such a trivial topic, he is influencing implicitly that the 'race card' is yet again being played, causing anger in viewers and further alienating people to the Black Lives Matter movement which highlights realistic important issues. All while he professes to support the movement.

Another fine example from *Good Morning Britain*: Piers Morgan has four people on a segment titled, 'Can white people recognise racism?'

The first video shown is of Black people protesting in London over the killing of George Floyd: it took place during the Covid-19 pandemic and it's clear that they are not observing social distancing. He asks one of the young ladies on the panel what she thinks about the fact they are breaking social distancing rules. Now, what has that question got to do with recognising racism? Suggesting they don't deserve our empathy given that they are acting so lawlessly. I wouldn't have a problem if the topic of discussion was actually around people breaking social distancing rules, but it was presented under the guise that they would be discussing racism when really it was a subliminal way of attacking those Black Lives Matters protestors and therefore making viewers angry and lose empathy, while also negating the message behind the protests.

I've always said that the detail, not the headline or shock of any story is the most important thing when coming to a conclusion about events. For example, a headline, 'John Barnes said Liam Neeson deserves a medal for wanting to kill a Black person.' No, he didn't. He said, 'Liam Neeson deserves a medal for realising how wrong he was to have such negative thoughts about people of a different group. How he felt ashamed and appalled by his thoughts (not actions), sought help from his priest, internalised his negative destructive thoughts realising that they were harming him, then after a week never had those thoughts again.' If only more people would do the same in being honest with themselves about their true feelings towards not only Black people but so many other groups who are disenfranchised by mainstream society, then the world truly would be a better place. Sadly, in this example, the negative and attacking response to Liam Neeson's honesty demonstrates perfectly why people are afraid to acknowledge how they feel, even if they know it's wrong, for fear of going through what him and others like him have experienced.

Another example of how sensationalism, headlines and focus unconsciously influences us, is the Winston Churchill narrative. If we wax lyrical about how fantastic he was during the war and give glowing reports on his exploits, then only throw in at the end that he did have a few flaws, of course people will see him as a perfect hero. As opposed to if we were to instead highlight his atrocities, failures and bigoted actions in detail (e.g. advocating the use of poisonous gas against the Kurds after World War I, the Bengal famine, treatment of the Mau Mau in Kenya, his 'Keep England White' slogan, to name just a few) then end with, 'well he was okay during World War II in keeping spirits up until the US and Russia joined us to win the war', then our perception of him would be very different.

PITTING ONE GROUP AGAINST ANOTHER

Consider hypothetically a working-class white boy from Liverpool, living in a single-parent home with a poor education, and compare him to a working-class Black boy in Liverpool from a single-parent household with a poor education. We can quite confidently say that the white boy would be more likely to succeed than the Black boy.

'They are persevering and getting on with it despite having negative outcomes, so why can't Black people!' I hear said sometimes. What I take from that comment is that those other groups, instead of saying, 'we get on with it, so should you', should say, 'hang on a minute, if you're saying we are more disenfranchised and discriminated against than Black people, who are ALSO discriminated against (whether less or more is a separate debate), then we should demand and protest as strongly as Black people are for equal opportunities!'. So why don't they? They don't, and this is where the book comes full circle for me, because for a thousand years, the non-elite have thought, 'THIS IS IT . . . more equality, justice and respect for us is near', only for their hopes to be dashed after a short period of time and the status quo to be reinstated with a few but no significant changes being achieved. Many people in those groups have given up hope and stopped not only demanding more for themselves, but even wanting or insisting on more visible representation of people like them in the hope that their representatives will help them up the ladder or inspire them to greatness.

The two most urgent, demanding and threatening forms of equality to challenge the status quo in the last few years, have been racial and gender equality. But gender gets relegated to not only below racial inequality, but also class, geography and home life in terms of expected and more deserving outcomes. This creates a huge dilemma: class, geography and family dynamics pertaining to disadvantages in society leading to negative outcomes has been an ongoing discussion for much longer than the current race discussion (as we know it today), and yet these issues haven't even begun to be properly addressed to change the balance. With the racial discourse now being put below those problems on the long agenda (God help women, they are below us on the list!), how many hundreds of years will it be before we revisit the racial question, never mind the gender question?

People who deny there is an issue will always point to evidence and statistics to back up their claims, e.g. Black kids stabbing Black kids, more Black people than white in prison, poorer exam results for Afro-Caribbean boys, etc. Our response to this is to explain that those are their skewed statistics and findings, to support their narrative because of their background.

11

SCAPEGOATS? LET'S LOOK AT OURSELVES FIRST . . .

As I have mentioned many times before, our current tactic of pointing the finger at individuals who display overt acts of racial bias or discrimination rather than introspectively looking at ourselves is only helping us to remain completely static in where we are with regard to race relations and discrimination as a wider issue. Below I will discuss a mere few of those who have been used as scapegoats. These stories highlight issues and opinions that many people in our society have likely felt and may even openly agree with; we punish these individuals rather than trying to address the reasons behind their actions in a non-judgemental way and therefore do not really get to the issues at hand.

In June 2020, US Navy captain Scott Bethmann and his wife were caught making racist remarks while unaware they were being recorded. After the video went viral, he explained that he was appalled at their behaviour, so shocked that normal and well-respected people like themselves have been racially biased. They were overheard complaining about no longer being able to make jokes and stated, 'the white m***** f***** can't say anything these days!' Many white people feel the same these days but are afraid to express that opinion for fear of being called racist. He says that he has grown and learnt from his experience, something we've heard from people many times before. But like the majority, what he has learnt is how to be more careful and not get caught rather than thinking about the reason he said what he did in the first place.

A young white woman named Amy Cooper was caught up in a scandal in Central Park regarding her interaction with a Black man, Christian Cooper, a birdwatcher and a Marvel comic editor, while walking her dog. She was asked politely by Christian Cooper to put her dog on a lead as per the rules in the park. It was not an unusual request by any means, but she felt slighted by this and reacted indignantly towards the man, shouting at him and calling the police to say she was being threatened by him, which was not at all the case in reality. She automatically understood the dynamic of what it means to call the police on a Black man and felt that he would be intimidated by that act. She thought he would then back down, knowing what we all know in terms of police interactions with Black people. However, he was not intimidated, stood his ground and she ended up with egg on her face.

On the very same day, just a few hours later in another state, the murder of George Floyd took place. Being a left wing, liberal, Obama-supporting, Trump-hating Democrat, I'm sure Amy Cooper would have been on the front lines of the Black Lives Matter movement protests, had she not been involved with this scandal. What caused her to act in that way? Like the majority of people in times of stress and confrontation, our unconscious mind takes over and makes us see our opponent in terms of hierarchy, be it racial, gender, religious or otherwise, and our attack on that person is dictated by our perception of their worthiness compared to ours. Had it been a white, upper-class businessman who politely asked her this same question she would have reacted in a very different way. This in no way was a conscious attack on Amy Cooper, but just like at times when some football fans racially abuse Black opposition players, while idolising their own Black players, unconscious bias came to the fore.

Another story to add to the long list of scapegoats who have let their racial bias show in public and receive national backlash is the story of twenty-four-year-old Sharna Walker, who in May 2021 was caught on video outside a nightclub in Birmingham shouting racial abuse, physically pushing and spitting at a Black bouncer after not being allowed back into the club. The video of course went viral and there was uproar from people claiming how shocking it is to see someone, especially a young person, using such language and acting in that way in public with what seemed to be no shame. Sharna shared an apology on her Instagram page claiming she is a good person and was just drunk. In the statement she asks for forgiveness and says she is entitled to free speech, even stating, 'I am in fact no racist at all, I have several Black co-workers who I love dearly and have even dated Black men.'

I have already discussed in the book why this oh-so-commonly used argument of 'but I have Black friends!' does not stand up as evidence that you don't have racial bias, but what I really want to highlight here again is not necessarily the actions of Sharna Walker but the response from society. How many times will we make an example of someone, call them a racist, be shocked and appalled at their behaviour and use it to make us feel great about ourselves because 'we would never do anything like that!' So completely ignoring the root of the issue and not considering that most likely, a huge number of people in our communities have those internal unconscious feelings and maybe this is something we should try to address and change.

Professor Greg Paton at the University of Southern California was suspended for using a word that sounded like 'nigger' in a class about pause and filler words used in different languages. The word he used in Mandarin is 'nei ge'.

My son Jamie, who is a doctor, had a Chinese colleague who he heard speaking to her parents in Cantonese, and also heard her saying 'nei ge'. He asked her what she was saying, and his colleague replied that it is a common word used in China, equivalent to the possessive pronoun 'your' in English.

Professor Paton's class was concerned with filler words and sounds in different languages/cultures. I find it ridiculous that so many Black university students should take offence. It gives ammunition to those who accuse us once again of 'playing the race card about everything'.

Here we are now demanding the Chinese change a word that they have been using for thousands of years because it sounds like a word that became offensive to Black people in the last two hundred years.

Just like telling the Romanian fourth official that 'ala negru' should not be used because it sounds like 'negro', and that he should have sensitivity training. Let me explain. During a Champions League match between Paris St Germain and Istanbul Basaksehir in December 2020, play was suspended. It was alleged that the Romanian fourth official, in describing Basaksehir's assistant coach (Pierre Webo) to the referee in order for the latter to send him off, had used the term 'ala negru' (translation: 'the Black guy'). Webo was the only Black coach amongst five or six other white coaches all wearing similar tracksuits. The accusations were of racism.

What has not been widely focused on is why the fourth official was concerned enough to involve the referee. You can watch the clip on YouTube. Allegedly, the referee and his assistants could hear cries of 'gypsies' coming from the sidelines. That is why the fourth official called over the referee in the first place.

So, what are Romanians supposed to feel towards Black people when one of their own is being vilified for saying 'the Black guy', but the initial investigation appeared to overlook the comment about 'gypsies'? I feel like we are told that we cannot say 'coloured' but describing us as 'Black' is acceptable, so why was the fourth official in trouble for saying 'the Black guy'?

Amber Rudd, at the time government's Work and Pensions Secretary, was giving a speech about the struggle women were having in politics to be accepted by society, and she went on to say that 'coloured' women have an even harder time. Labour MP Diane Abbott, instead of thanking her for pointing out the fact that Black women do have a harder time but that the term should be 'Black' not 'coloured', called for her to resign because she used the wrong word. Amber Rudd was supporting Black women and their struggles, but because she used the wrong term, she was lambasted, and the necessary conversation around female (Black and white) inequality was lost because the debate was now about her using an inappropriate word. Former Liverpool and BBC football pundit Alan Hansen said that 'coloured players' were great and brought so much to the game, and rather than saying thanks for the compliment Black people called for him to be sacked because he said 'coloured'. I actually said to him that he should have said 'Black players are shit' (I was obviously only being facetious) as he wouldn't have got into trouble because he got the terminology right.

FA Chairman Greg Clarke also got into trouble while support-ing Black and gay footballers and was forced to resign because his terminology was wrong even though his intentions were laudable. I say this to all the younger people today who use language rather than intention as a stick to beat people with: in thirty years' time, when acceptable language may change once again and terms used today aren't considered okay, even though they might use those terms with the right intention, they might be cancelled out by tomorrow's children for being out of touch with the times.

As we were putting the finishing touches to the book, I had discussions with the publishers regarding issues of sensitivity, and the possibility of causing offence to different groups of people when covering problematic subjects.

I feel it is appropriate in this day and age for that process to have been followed, not least because it is clear how issues like the ones discussed in this book can affect people.

This section came under more scrutiny than most, and the discussion centred around what we might call language that was acceptable in years gone by, but that may not be acceptable today. You will have noticed that I wrote *may* not be acceptable today. Why not *definitely wouldn't* be acceptable today? Well, because we have to consider the nuances and complications around what is and isn't acceptable, and more importantly by whom.

I am referring specifically to the word 'coloured' as mentioned above. While the term may be unacceptable in the UK, in South Africa it is not only acceptable but it is insisted on when talking about the separate race of 'coloured' people. That is why I say context and intent should always be considered before making a judgement.

Some may say: 'That's fine over there, but over here it shouldn't be used or accepted', and that may be the case if Black people insist on the term not being used towards them in this country. However, if a commentator here is commentating on a football match in which, for example, South Africans Benni McCarthy or Steven Pienaar are playing, then the commentator *should* identify them as 'coloured' and not 'Black', as those individuals themselves identify that way. Who are we to tell them they are wrong?

These scapegoats we create are not unique in their actions, they are like the average person who just got caught. There will be many more victims in the ongoing witch hunt, and sadly we find it easier to expose them in order to feel better about ourselves and avoid looking within to ask ourselves if we might be just like them – rather than being accountable for our own unconscious bias.

ACCOUNTABILITY

People say, 'Racism is bad, and I'm not a bad person so I can't be a racist. Stealing is wrong, I'd never steal, but if I could get a million pounds from someone who wouldn't miss it, and no one would get hurt then I might.' Now that is still stealing and it's still wrong, so what's the difference? The difference is one of those options is 'less' wrong. That concept is just like degrees of racism. Many people say they cannot understand why someone would be racist, but that type of statement alone is not bringing any solution. The real solution is to actually try to understand why someone is racist. If you don't know the reason behind why people are racist, you can't help them to change their views.

Is there a difference between racism and racial bias? We may admit to being racially biased but won't admit to being racist, as we see racists as people wearing pointy white hats, shouting abuse at footballers, policemen who stop, search and shoot Black people. So as long as that isn't us, we convince ourselves that we aren't racist. But is there a difference really?

It's claimed that modern Black football players or celebrities have bigger voices than their predecessors. I don't believe that is so, rather society just pretends to have bigger ears. What we hear a lot concerning scapegoats who have been 'caught' on social media for example and seem remorseful, is, 'What have they learnt?' The only thing society has learnt is how not to get caught. At times, they have used a Black elite person to tell them how not to get caught, for example by asking, 'Well, what type of language would be acceptable for me to use instead?' That means as long as we are not overtly offending anyone with words, our intent isn't accounted for, even if it is racially biased.

Gary Lineker reminded me recently, via Twitter, of the conversations we used to have as football players in the late '80s on the unconscious bias we all had. Conversations regarding his own, and other players', perceived acceptance of Black people because of their friendships with me and other Black players they knew relative to the perception of Black people they didn't know. His tweet was along the lines of, 'Still going on about the average man being racist', which is absolutely correct but let's instead say racially biased. This rings true because of the fact that the average man accepts the equality of his Black friends and counterparts, but not of the Black man he doesn't know.

Henry Bonsu, a Black journalist and broadcaster, was sacked by BBC London radio station because they claimed he didn't connect with listeners. Whose fault is that, the station or the listeners? We are led to believe that, in this case, it is the 'racist' radio station's decision to get rid of him. However, being a business, the radio station is only concerned with making money, so their sole aim is for the presenter to connect with the audience in order to keep as many listeners as possible. If he is not 'connecting', therefore receiving lower listener numbers, then is that the radio station's fault or the listeners' fault?

Rather than blaming the radio station we should look at ourselves as listeners and ask, why do feel we aren't connecting with him? We can also think about this concept with regard to the situation with *Good Morning Britain* following Piers Morgan's departure. This led to a huge drop in viewer numbers, so what was it about him that viewers were able to connect with him so much? While most people wouldn't admit it openly, it's obvious that not only does he have a big fanbase, but he is able to influence people's thoughts and perception.

LBC radio station recently addressed their lack of diversity all of a sudden by having *one* Black woman on for discussion and announced this will be a regular occurrence. Another visible example of tokenism which we, as Black people, will love because it appears things are getting better for the chosen one per cent. White presenters are now talking to their lesser

Black compatriots and saying 'now' they understand what they've been going through and only 'now' do they notice the lack of representation in their spaces. Wow, how long will either the acknowledgement or the concern last?

Chelsea Handler, a famous white American comedian and TV host, made a documentary about white privilege. Among many other interviews in the show, she spoke to a group of white middle-class women in Orange County, Southern California, about their feelings around this topic. One of the women interestingly said she believes in Black underprivilege but not white privilege. This makes no sense, because in admitting that there is Black underprivilege that means there MUST be such thing as white privilege. Something that they may consider to be a very average, normal outcome can be considered a privilege in the eyes of Black people and that's what has to be understood around this discussion.

It is important to keep using terms like white supremacy, white liberal and white society, because to address the problem, we have to identify the protagonists rather than just saying 'society'. Otherwise people will always think that the problem doesn't lie with them but with someone else. People need to be able to take accountability for themselves. The invisibility of white supremacy has been its greatest weapon, because society is convinced it doesn't exist any longer. We can discuss and critique capitalism, socialism, communism, etc. because it's visibly there to be judged. But how we do the same to an ideal that isn't even considered to be present anymore? We have to openly talk about these things.

Since most of society accepts class discrimination, I don't know what is so hard to accept about the fact that there is racial discrimination. We know full well the historical narrative surrounding Black people; we know how in the Enlightenment period the idea of superiority within the white race was spread to help to support slavery and colonialism by creating the idea of a group of 'less worthy' people whom the West could exploit.

People may say it's not important when it comes to the question of whether people would feel more empathy hearing about 400 teenage girls being kidnapped in Nigeria if they were blonde-haired, blue-eyed rather than Black girls. Many say that point is irrelevant as no matter how much empathy they feel, they still can't do anything about it. But there is a reason why it is in fact important to address that attitude; in those times when you do have the power to do something, be it employ someone, trust someone, believe one to be as worthy as the other, it's important you authentically see them as equal. It goes beyond just doing the right thing. You have to genuinely feel everyone is equally worthy of whatever you have to give, and not base your judgement of them on race, gender, religion or sexuality.

There are three types of people: people who are racists and know it, people who are racist but don't know or think they are (which is by far the largest group) and people who aren't racist at all. Now, if a Black footballer speaks out against racism, wears the Kick It Out T-shirt, etc., who does that have an effect on? The people who belong to the first group don't care and won't suddenly have an epiphany to stop being racist; the racist football fan will not act racist towards the Black player on his team but will continue to do so towards the Black opposition . . . so no change there. The people in the second group don't actually think they're racist so they feel it doesn't apply to them . . . no change there. Finally, the people in the third group don't need to change as they have no racial bias to start with . . . so overall nothing changes. What we need to do is to explain to people WHY it's wrong to be racist, and how we all became racially biased in the first place through unconscious conditioning.

What has changed recently in our lives for the 99 per cent of us who have suddenly woken up and now authentically believe in equality for all races, sexes, religion, etc? An enlightenment, epiphany or just a better understanding of how not to get caught? It's taken me years of introspection for me to finally, consciously, acknowledge my bias. While that doesn't mean I am able to necessarily change completely overnight, I make sure to always challenge myself rather than point the finger at the ones who get found out and pretend that they are the only culprits.

Our growth should be treated like a circle. There are degrees of bias: for example, a person who is aware of the biases that they hold but doesn't care to change as they truly believe they are superior, compared to a person holding an unconscious bias that they genuinely are unaware of so therefore can't see that there is anything that needs to change. Then it's back full circle to having conscious bias with a difference: we know we are biased, and that we are wrong, and we want to try to make a change. That final example should be the end goal for us all. Of course, in an ideal world we would have no biases at all, but this is extremely difficult at this stage in our progress.

The first step in the journey towards racial equality is acknowledgement that unconscious bias exists within all of us. Unfortunately, very few people are able to do this and instead go down the route of searching out the 'guilty people' and dealing with them. Now this may be the second or third step, which we have already been doing for many years, but you can't start a race on the second step, i.e. without looking introspectively first. I feel this is why we have only made limited progress in addressing this challenge.

12

ARE THINGS REALLY
DIFFERENT NOW?

I used to watch a lot of *Def Comedy Jam* videos from America, I'm a huge fan and think a lot of those comedians are hilarious: Black, politically incorrect comedians talking about life. Eddie Murphy, Jamie Foxx, Martin Lawrence, Chris Rock, Chris Tucker, Steve Harvey, Wanda Sykes, Cheryl Underwood – so many of them now mainstream comedians who were underground comedians back then, keeping it real. They would frequently talk about racial differences between white and Black, and although they would exaggerate for comedic effect, it resonated with both groups and to a certain degree we knew it to be true, no matter how crudely put. The comedians give examples of white people being so comfortable with their status in the world that they forget the laws of nature; they want to get out of their cars and take pictures of a lion on safari in Africa until it 'grabs their ass'. They regularly finish their examples with 'Black people don't do that', because 'don't we have enough bad luck happen to us in our lives than to go jump out of a plane, and swim with sharks?' They say, 'White people see a crowd running their way in a panic and run towards them to see what they runnin' from . . . Black people know if something bad is gonna happen to humans, they the first it gonna happen to.' They say when you read a story of an accident, depending on what it is, you know it's not a Black man, because 'we ain't jumpin' out no helicopter with just a pair of skis to ski down no mountain'. It's humour, but it is also truth. White people have been so empowered to know the world is their oyster, that they feel absolutely comfortable in doing anything because life has shown them that they can.

The king of comedians of course was Richard Pryor, and in my opinion the funniest stand-up video of all time is *Richard Pryor Live in Concert*. It is said that comedy is truth, and I believe that. How many times do we say things we mean, and if it causes offence add, 'Only joking', when truly we weren't? You can't get away with that these days, because you can't even 'joke' about discrimination (as if it doesn't exist). I'll give you some examples from Richard Pryor as to why comedy is truth.

Right from the start he says to his racially mixed audience, 'Nice to see you all. The white people are here first in an orderly fashion, whereas Black people turn up at the last minute and sit anywhere.' It works better with his accent and delivery but bear with me. He then talks about the white couple who go back to their seats after the intermission to find Black people sitting in them. The white couple will politely say that these are their seats, and they were sitting there earlier and just went to the bathroom during the intermission. The response from the Black guy is, 'Well, you ain't sitting here now m***** f*****', to which the white guy would say, 'No problem man.' When his wife says to him quietly that he should have stuck up for himself, he tells her off because there were loads of them and 'they could be related or anything'.

He tells stories of his life, one in particular about the way police treat Black people in LA, saying that they have a choke hold 'that can break a nigger'. He breaks off to ask the audience if they knew that the police had this choke hold 'that can break a nigger', then sharp as a flash follows with, 'All the white people are shakin' their heads sayin' . . . "no, I didn't know that", while all the Black people are nodding their heads saying, "Yeah! We know that."' Just shows how reality can differ for people living in the same place.

I think it was Martin Lawrence, the American comedian, actor and writer, who spoke about how hard it must have been in times of slavery, when you were completely subservient to the 'massa' and then spoke about how some of his 'boys' while watching *Roots*, the TV show about slaves in America, would say, 'I wouldn't be no slave, and I'd tell massa to suck my dick', in a hard Brooklyn accent. He then spoke of the reality in which the overseers whip would immediately tear the skin off your back, and in a Southern slave accent says, 'How many bales of cotton you gonna need today, massa?' So poking fun at the reality of how any of us would feel and act under such dire circumstances, no matter how tough we think we are today.

POLITICAL CORRECTNESS

A white ex-footballer friend of mine, who currently works in the media, called me up to say that they were now being told what words they can and can't use to describe Black players; LAZY was one of the banned words, THICK was another. It would upset Black players if they were called lazy, as that was what Black people were wrongly called for years just for being Black. The example that was used was when Ron Atkinson, who isn't any more or less racist than anyone of his time, called

Marcel Desailly a 'lazy, thick, f***ing nigger'. And the offensive word that was taken from that insult was LAZY.

If a Black player loses the ball and doesn't run back, anyone is well within their rights to call him LAZY, as they would do to a white player. If he makes a stupid decision on the field, he can be described in that moment as being THICK or STUPID (as would be said of a white player in similar circumstances) without there being any racial meaning behind it. Are we then saying that there can't be any negative words used, even by fans, when talking about Black players, because they may be deemed to be racist? Once again, INTENT is the most important thing, and if the intent is to describe a player's attitude, commitment or decisions on the pitch as lazy, stupid or arrogant, and he happens to be Black, this shouldn't become an issue.

I read a story about Everton fans singing a racist song a racist song about Yerry Mina, their Black, Columbian centre back on loan from Barcelona. It was after he had made a mistake in a match, so I assumed the song was criticising him. But it wasn't, it was about the misguided perception people have about Black men – the size of his manhood. It also included the tongue-in-cheek (maybe because it had to rhyme) perception of Colombians and cocaine. I'm sure Yerry Mina isn't in need of our sympathy and support, and they were actually praising him.

Agatha Christie wrote a book called *Ten Little Niggers*. Now that the use of the 'n' word is no longer acceptable, some people have called for all of her books to be banned and that she be stripped of whatever honours were bestowed upon her. Why didn't anyone bat an eyelid when she first titled that book? Because that was the way it was back then, and it's not fair to judge many things that happened in the past by today's standards. (The novel was subsequently retitled *And Then There Were None*.)

SOCIETY MUST CHANGE ITSELF

I'm hearing more and more the phrase that 'young Black people have had enough'. Do you not think that older Black people have endured much more in their lifetime and also have had more than enough? It gives people a sense of superiority to feel that they're doing more to change things than their predecessors did. You can do nothing alone to change society: society has to change of its own accord.

The Western world is like Monty Python's *Life of Brian*, in which you have the People's Front of Judea, the Popular Front, the Popular Peoples' Front, the People's Popular Front, and the Suicide Squad all fighting the Romans, and subsequently themselves. Only to end up all killing each other while Rome survives. Remember the scene where two groups were about to capture the senator's wife and make demands, but instead bumped into each other and started arguing about whose demands were more important, then ending up killing each other while the guards looked on. I use this example to demonstrate how different minority or disenfranchised groups can sometimes end up so embroiled in arguments or competition between themselves that they forget about the original and important goal of fighting against the establishment to achieve changes and create equal opportunities for themselves. The establishment is happy to encourage this behaviour as long as it distracts people from the real issues.

The vast majority of Black elite people believe that they are approaching the fight for equality in the right way, without understanding that throughout history this has happened many times before without success.

ACTIVISTS WHO SUCCESSFULLY FOUGHT
THE TIDE OF RACISM

There has been many activists in the fight against racism over the last 400 years, but here I want to give special mention to three in particular – Nelson Mandela, Martin Luther King, Jr and Mahatma Gandhi – because of their commitment, support, method and message to society concerning equal rights.

All three were brilliant, successful, powerful men, who, if they were to follow the direction of some of our leaders today, would have advocated for a more visible, representative and inclusive Black elite at the top of society . . . but they didn't.

Nelson Mandela, as a lawyer in South Africa, could have said, 'WE NEED MORE BLACK LAWYERS', as could Gandhi in India. Martin Luther King, Jr could have said that we need more Black business leaders and politicians in the higher echelons of mainstream society . . . but he didn't. They ALL believed that the way forward was to get justice, support, respect and equality for the most disadvantaged members of society.

Gandhi is interesting in another way, and here is a great example of how we have all been conditioned regarding racial hierarchies over time to think in terms of who is more worthy even among people of colour. He was educated as a lawyer in London, so had a Western education, and we know what that looks like. He was a brilliant lawyer, so he knew that although he was Indian, he was as worthy and intelligent as any white lawyer out there . . . consequently he knew that people like him, meaning other Indians, under the right circumstances, had the potential to be as moral or intelligent as any white person. However, when he went to South Africa to work and saw the way his people (Indians) were being treated, he was horrified that they were thought of as being the same as what he called 'Black savages', who he felt were inferior human beings. He called them 'kaffirs' and was horrified that the South African government wanted to allow the kaffirs to live in the same areas in which the Indians lived.

There are many quotes from him and stories of him show-ing utter contempt for Black people, but Gandhi was a great believer in equal rights for HIS OWN PEOPLE. That goes to show how unconscious conditioning affects even the most right-minded and intelligent of us, and if a great man like Gandhi can be influenced by what he has been wrongly told about different groups of people . . . what chance does the average person have?

EQUAL OPPORTUNITIES

Black people and women are equally as good as white men at swimming, but they are metaphorically swimming against the tide. There is no point in putting them in the same race unless we change the tide. Now, there will always be a few excellent Black people and excellent women who, despite the tide, will finish equal or above white men, but all that does is convince people that the tide doesn't exist, and that argument is actually counterproductive in the fight for equal opportunities.

When Jesse Owens won the gold medal for America in the 1936 Olympic 100-metre sprint there were very few Black athletes taking part. The semi-finals and final were mainly white athletes. Nowadays, and for the last few decades, athletics at the Olympics has been mainly dominated by Black athletes. So, the question is, have Black people got faster since the early 1900s? Or is there now an environment created for them to not only maximise their physical potential, but also be allowed to compete? There likely would have been many other Black athletes around in the early 1900s who, if allowed and if the environment was conducive for them to maximise their potential, could have been present in that 100-metre final alongside Jesse Owens.

Great British gymnasts in the 1970s would have had the same potential as the modern GB gymnasts of the 2012 or 2016 Olympics, but because there wasn't an environment created to help them maximise their potential, they didn't win many medals back then. So, we thought they weren't good enough. Meanwhile, in East Germany and Russia the climate was tailored for them to achieve success and that's why they dominated, not necessarily because they were better, just that the opportunities in that discipline were superior.

In a similar vein, women have always had the inherent ability and potential to be heads of huge corporations, but the environment thirty or forty years ago did not encourage them to show their worth and achieve this. Women today aren't necessarily better, more intelligent or more able than the women of the past, but the environment is changing to increase their opportunities and encourage them to reach different goals.

In football management, until there is an environment created to give opportunities to Black managers, allowing trust, belief and time, then there will only be the odd one or two who are afforded opportunities but not the vast majority. However, as opposed to the previous argument about athletes, there is a much bigger challenge facing Black managers. Physical sport is easy to dissect: fastest wins, strongest wins, it's obvious and undeniable. So, when people say it's only a matter of time for the transition of the Black players of today to then become managers, it's not as simple as that. Because management is about leadership, intellect, organisation and other 'skills' that Black people generally aren't perceived to have. Until we change society's perception of Black people's morality, intellect and leadership qualities BEFORE they are even given these management opportunities, nothing will change. If they are given these opportunities BEFORE we change those widely held, usually unconscious, perceptions then unless they win most or all matches, the unconscious negative perceptions will rear their ugly head to ask, 'Are they really good enough for the job?'

Ultimately, the solution is to create a climate for disadvantaged groups to maximise their potential: give them time, support, trust and belief rather than looking at one or two people in a non-supportive environment that doesn't provide real opportunities. The fact that the 100-metre sprint final at the next Olympics will likely have seven Black athletes compared to the early 1900s with seven white athletes (apart from those representing Black countries of course) is proof of what creating opportunities can do.

13

FACING THE FUTURE: INTROSPECTION AND HONESTY

How do we re-condition our minds to be anti-racist? In the same way we originally became conditioned to think in terms of racial, gender or sexual hierarchy – through constant continued influences and debate, subliminally and implicitly. I understand why people are cautious about having honest, meaningful discussions on discrimination, because if we do, we could easily be accused of discrimination ourselves. But we have to be brave and face this.

Empathy with racists is needed because they are also victims of indoctrination, just like detectives and criminal profilers who try to empathise with serial killers to allow them to understand why and how they operate, therefore gaining the ability to stop them. Empathy here is not just about understanding people's pain and suffering, but also their greed and exploitative ways.

If Western civilisation wants to try to move forward, we should look at the reasoning behind the Peace and Reconciliation programme in Rwanda after the genocide in 1994, which I have discussed earlier in the book. That programme wasn't about finding out who was guilty in particular, because some of the people who were involved were also victims who had been forced to take part or they themselves would have been killed. Instead, it was about an honest acknowledgement of what people had done, without fear of being judged too harshly, an acknowledgement that they weren't completely innocent. The truth and reconciliation process made people accountable for their actions, in order for them to recognise their heinous actions and to make it less likely that they might do such things or behave in such ways again.

Nowadays there is a drive in both America and Britain to get rid of tributes to many heroic historical figures of the past (e.g. statues) because of what they stand for now. I understand the feeling people have towards them now, but they were heroes of that age, misguided or not, and the views they held were largely the same as the majority of the people at that time.

It doesn't bother me one way or the other whether their statues are removed or not, but I think it could serve as a reminder of the discrimination of the past, without judgement so that it may not happen again. Without those reminders, mistakes and perceptions of the past may be tangibly forgotten, so there may be no accountability for the present or future as the visible proof will have been erased.

On the subject of statues, a few hundred yards from where my mother lives in central Kingston, Jamaica, a statue was commissioned in a park to celebrate when the slaves came to Jamaica to make it the country that it is now. There was huge anticipation to see this large statue of a proud, Black naked African . . . but to the astonishment of all my family members as well as many other Jamaicans, not only was he well sculptured and magnificent but he had a HUGE PENIS! Of course, this park would forever become known as 'Penis Park'. The question to be asked is: why did we as Black Jamaicans feel the need to have to demonstrate that not only do we have all those qualities that the world leaders have, but also a bigger manhood? We complain about the stereotyping of the Black man, then we go and do this? Had this statue been commissioned in the UK or US, I shudder to think what Black people would have made of those WHITE people stereotyping US.

While the big penis may seem like a physical reality of the strong Black man, it really is a metaphor for the only sign, visible or otherwise, for the only manly representation that wasn't or couldn't be taken away from the completely emasculated male slave.

Now, what I'm hearing from society is that we must learn more about Black history and culture. No, society needs to learn more about its own history and culture to understand how we got to this position of such unconscious superiority and inferiority. Your position is not based on moral, intellectual and altruistic superiority, it's based on greed, violence and theft.

Imagine two scenarios. The first one: everyone in society has the same amount and are equal. The second one: a minority have the most and the majority have less. Which sounds better? One is called socialism and the other is called capitalism. Because of the historical stigma attached to the word socialism, the narrative concerning that ideology is frowned upon. So, what's wrong with socialism? Nothing. But it can never work because of mankind's greed. In that case, shouldn't the solution be to try to reduce our greediness and change the environment that promotes and supports this? I'm no different, and while I still can't help but crave what I feel I deserve, do I really want it to the detriment of others in my society? No. But I understand that the only way for me to get it in this environment, IS to the detriment of others. So, do I want a social revolution? No, it's too late for that. I think we as humans (myself included) have become too greedy for that to work. We always want more than the next man, which is why socialism or communism as we know it has always failed, even when started with the right intention. What I do want is a more balanced society based on merit, not race, gender, sexuality or religion.

The only way to truly destroy racism is to destroy capitalism. Even if we create so-called equality for Black people, by the very nature of a capitalist society there will always be others who are exploited. The only way to achieve true equality for all is by creating a socialist society, and that's not about to happen whether we think it should or not. For the majority to have more than they do now (economically, socially, or in matters of respect), it means our elite minority (who control the system and make all decisions regarding political and social change) will have to have less. If they are prepared to do so, it can work . . . but are they? The answer is unfortunately a big fat NO!

The success of a society should be the happiness, worth and equality of its average person, not the success of a few elites.

Take the record breaking 2018 film *Black Panther* as an example. When looking at this film, the success of the Black characters should not be judged on the fact that they have extravagant, superior technology and weapons compared to the rest of the world, but that the community in which they live, Wakanda, shows average citizens living with respect, opportunities, a good quality of life and self-worth for all.

Visible diversity, rather than cultural or philosophical diversity, is a useful tool. This allows us to empathise with those different groups of people we see, or work with. And this visibility has to include seeing that person in the Western world we live in, not just the cultural or philosophical world of the other people who look like them, to allow us to be able to relate to them and have understanding.

Society's take on racism reminds me of a football match, with regard to the response from fans compared to the response of the managers. The managers will all talk about the 'performance', meaning the full ninety minutes and not just the 'highlights' which is what the fans rave about. When we watch the highlights, we see two goals and a handful more exciting moments; it doesn't represent the true full story of the game. You can win a game 2–0 by having only two shots on target where the opposition may have had twenty-five shots, hit the bar ten times, have five cleared off the line but still lost. So, managers say the performance is more important than the result. Because if you continue to play in a way where you achieve twenty-five shots on goal and five cleared off the line, you will eventually score more goals and win more games, despite the fact you lost this one. How does this equate to the fight against racism? Well, if we keep focusing on the 'highlights' only (George Floyd, Amy Cooper, the odd football fan) and feel that in doing so we are winning the fight, what we are actually doing is being the team who gets only two shots on target. We need to stop neglecting the whole 'performance' which at present looks like inequality for the majority of Black people in terms of jobs, education, social services, exploitation, crime, housing and a host of other examples where racial bias has an effect. Improving the overall 'performance' in the wider society is the only way we will truly have any hope of achieving equality.

Re-education of the people has to involve total change to the long-held view of our society. Looking at examples of attempts at mass re-education in history such as Pol Pot, Chairman Mao, the Chinese with the Uighurs, we see that educated people are always the ones who are targeted to silence as they are seen as too far influenced and conditioned to truly change (you can't teach an old dog new tricks). So, what do the evil despots of the past have to do with racism/discrimination? Not much, it's more an example as to why our belief that changing things from within, by infiltrating into an existing system, has never worked regardless of right or wrong, good or evil.

Pol Pot, the Cambodian communist revolutionary who was the driving force behind the genocide in the 1970s, as evil as he was, recognised that the way the Cambodian elite had been conditioned (consciously or unconsciously) was so irreversible, endemic and contagious that 're-education' would be futile. They considered themselves to be the more intelligent of the Cambodians and therefore could be unmoved by indoctrination. To overcome this issue, he decided to just kill them all. How could he have been able to identify which people were the capitalist conditioned intelligentsia (not necessarily wealthy, just educated)? He had only a short space of time to make his revolution successful before outside forces, with the help of remaining Cambodian elite, tried to retake power. These decisions, as to whether you were intelligent (therefore conditioned, based on the Western world's view on worthiness and intelligence), were made by characteristics as simple as, 'If you wear glasses, you can read . . . if you can read you have been educated . . . if you are educated, you are lost to the possibility to change your perceptions.' Pol Pot didn't have time to work out who was who, so he decided to kill most people who had glasses, and the same applied to most people who spoke French, as they would be considered intelligent as well. It's not that he necessarily hated intelligent people, he would have considered himself intelligent, it was people who he considered TOO intelligent to influence and change. Pol Pot also knew that he had to use children to his advantage, as they can be easily influenced and conditioned to carry out punishment. This is the same in Afghanistan, Myannmar, Yemen and some African countries who horrifically enlist children as soldiers to do their violent work.

Chairman Mao, the Chinese communist revolutionary and the founding father of the People's Republic of China, used a similar technique for cultural revolution. Schools and universities were closed to 're-educate' people in the way he felt was right, millions of the intelligentsia were imprisoned, and the idea of everyone 'working the land for the greater good' was indoctrinated into society.

There have been many attempts over the years to adopt similar philosophies whereby a group of the wider community revolt and try to infiltrate the leadership system, albeit not to the extent of the previous two examples I have used. However, Cuba managed it (to their detriment, although they have survived), Venezuela have and continue to try it but are struggling, and myriad of other developing countries have attempted it usually unsuccessfully. The only reason North Korea are surviving at present is because of the support and protection from China. Now, this isn't a lecture on politics, socialism, communism, good or evil, right or wrong; it's just explaining why our Black perspective of 'we need to get into the system to be able to make change', in my opinion, won't work. It never has. All of the previous examples, and there are many more over the last thousand years, have been unsuccessful because the only thing that changes in all the revolutions is that there is increased wealth and power bestowed upon certain individuals within that revolutionary group. And time and time again those individuals then go on to continue the exploitation of the masses, the people who they originally purported to be representing in the first place.

Trying to change the educational curriculum here in the UK alone isn't enough in the system that exists. So, the answer is not just about what we teach in history, but about how we can change the narrative of those historical events to give a more accurate explanation. We need to recondition people to see things more clearly than they do now regarding themselves and others.

In conclusion, I feel that things may be getting worse. In addition to the official Sewell Report on systemic racism in the UK that I discussed earlier in the book, there is another official report released by the Education Select Committee of the House of Commons which states that the term 'white privilege' is now not applicable and doesn't exist due to the fact that white working-class people are not privileged. As if they are a separate ethnic group to the white middle and upper classes? It has never been suggested that white working-class people are privileged, but the establishment has always pushed back against that term by using them to deny the fact that white people generally have more opportunities than other groups. Well now they have an official report to prove their case. They state that it's divisive to talk about or suggest the idea of 'white privilege'. When it was more obviously detrimental to other groups in years gone by, this 'divisiveness' was never considered, because it favoured white society, as it still does. Does that mean that addressing sexism or homophobia is also 'divisive', or is it just that we go on about race too much? If we were to demand less, I imagine we would get a more favourable outcome.

We are turning our 'neutral' white allies into allies of the enemy, which leads me to question their allyship in the first place. Just like with the BLM movement, people push back by saying, 'Now it just stands for tearing down statues and defunding the police, so maybe you should come up with a different name and ideology to gain wider support.' So, we must come up with something different for 'white privilege' so as not to offend? These suggestions are being proposed by people purporting to be our allies. While they ascertain that they themselves do understand that footballers taking a knee aren't necessarily just supporting the tearing down of statues and defunding the police, and the term white privilege is separate to white working-class underprivilege, they tell us that because there are others who don't understand this, we should come up with something else. If they understand and acknowledge it, shouldn't they try to convince the others to do the same? Assure the wider community that the narratives of 'Black lives mattering' and 'white privilege' do exist.

Something that is truly divisive, and we all have heard and used the term 'divide and conquer' especially with regard to the disenfranchised groups, is using those very same exploited groups against each other instead of encouraging them to come together in support against an elitist establishment. This is why, as I've said all along, before we pass any laws on equality and discrimination, we have to fight to be 'seen' as equal as a race of people, and 'worthy' of not being discriminated against, rather than looking to enshrine in policy the legality of equality and inclusivity.

For the last 200 years, our 'allies' (abolitionists, and opponents to colonialism) have fought for the legal and moral rights of enfranchisement, but that always was from THEIR perspective, for their own retribution and right-mindedness. They didn't consider for one second whether they actually perceived Black people as intellectually or morally equal. In fact, the vast majority of them back then didn't feel that Black people were equal, but just knew it was wrong to treat these 'unequal' people in such terrible ways.

We can use the white working-class community as an example as to why we should strive to 'see people as equal' before just 'appearing to treat them as equal'. They haven't been seen as equal by the upper echelons for over a thousand years, so there is no need or demand to treat them as equal nowadays, although there might have been at the beginning. Years ago, they may have demanded equality from the elite but had no success and therefore 'accepted' their fate and continued to live in underprivileged ways with no sign of change.

This is not the way it should be, but unfortunately it is the situation we as a society are in. We, as Black people, will end up with the same fate if we don't change our approach and fight to be truly seen as equal first rather than being handed out a few pitiful dregs and just being paid lip service to in the short term. Albert Einstein is credited with the saying, 'The definition of insanity is doing the same thing over and over again but expecting different results.' We have been doing that for years regarding race relations, so is there any wonder that we are not making progress?

If we ever achieve racial equality, it won't mean that there are no more poor, exploited and disenfranchised Black people. Some people may remain all of those things, but the difference will be that those underprivileges will not be occurring because of their skin colour, but because of other factors in life. This is because, as I have discussed previously, there will always be differences in the privileges and lifestyles of people in communities, unless we aim for a full socialist system which would be impossible, but what we should be aiming for is that those differences are not happening to people because of their race.

Moving forward, I will continue in my efforts, as difficult as they may be, to work on introspection and address my own internal unconscious biases in a non-judgemental way. I will use my platform to highlight what I feel are the true barriers to equality, in terms of racial, gender, religious, sexuality and class-based factors.

I hope that in reading this book you will be encouraged to debate and consider all of these topics with family, friends, colleagues, even strangers. We need to open up the discussion, be brave and honest, and hope that we, as individuals, can do our small part in changing the perceptions of society.